MW01042043

VISUAL QUICKSTART GUIDE

NETSCAPE 2

FOR MACINTOSH

Elizabeth Castro

Peachpit Press

Visual QuickStart Guide
Netscape 2 for Macintosh
Elizabeth Castro

Peachpit Press
2414 Sixth Street
Berkeley, CA 94710
(510) 548-4393
(510) 548-5991 (fax)

Find us on the World Wide Web at: http://www.peachpit.com

Peachpit Press is a division of Addison Wesley Longman

Cover design: The Visual Group

Notice of liability

The information in this book is distributed on an "As is" basis, without warranty. While every precaution has been taken in the preparation of this book, neither the author nor Peachpit Press shall have any liability to any person or entity with respect to any loss or damage caused or alleged to be caused directly or indirectly by the instructions contained in this book or by the computer software and hardware products described herein.

ISBN: 0-201-88631-6

0 9 8 7 6 5 4 3 2 1

✿ Printed on recycled paper

Printed in the United States of America

For Becky and Jenny who taught me my multiplication tables,
my Uncle Myron Pollyea who taught me exponential powers,
and Stephen Ucich, my first (and only) computer teacher.

Special thanks to:

Kaethin Prizer, Kate Reber, and **Nolan Hester** at Peachpit Press
for their great suggestions and corrections, and for their calm replies
to frantic, last minute questions.

The folks who frequent the **netscape.navigator** newsgroup
and who seem to know all the answers.

Andreu, for everything else.

Table of Contents

Introduction

The beauty—and the peril—of the World Wide Web is that everyone can publish their own information quickly and easily. As such, the Web is the fastest growing area in the computer world today. Each month thousands of new pages are added, by huge companies and private citizens alike.

Some pages are serious collections of commercial information. Others are personal accounts of travels, history, and life itself. Still others attempt to fill the void that the paper publishing industry is unable to answer. Perhaps the nicest thing about the Web is that there are pages about everything, from cancer research to bowling, from solar panel design to hot new bands.

What is the Web, really?

The Internet is a huge collection of computers that are connected to each other. Some computers are connected to the Internet through a telephone and modem (and are thus only *on* the Internet when they are connected). Other computers are permanently connected (generally, universities and large companies fall into this category).

There are different ways of communicating over the Internet, called *protocols*. E-mail is the most common protocol, but you may have heard of FTP, Gopher, Usenet, and HTTP, as well. This last protocol, HTTP, is the method computers use to connect to each other and view Web pages.

What is a Web page?

A Web page is nothing more than a text document with special tags. These tags add formatting, images, and hypertext links to the page. But because a Web page is a text document, in ASCII format, it can be opened on virtually any platform, from Macintosh to Windows, and including everything in between.

Although you could open a Web page with a text editor, the special tags are not interpreted unless you open the page with a browser. There are many different kinds of browsers, with different versions of each for each kind of computer platform.

Netscape Navigator 2

Netscape Navigator 2 is the most popular browser, used by some 70% of the Web public. Commonly known as Netscape (but *not* Navigator), the new version of the software combines a first-class browser with news and mail capabilities.

This book is divided into three principal sections: *The World Wide Web* (for browsing the Web), *Mail and News* (for e-mail and newsgroups), and *Preferences* (for customizing Netscape).

What is a Web page?

Part I:
The World Wide Web

11

The Web Browser

Figure 1.1 *Choose New Web Browser in the File menu to open a new browser.*

Figure 1.2 *A fresh browser opens. It may or may not be empty, depending on your settings.*

Figure 1.3 *Choose Close in the File menu to make the browser disappear.*

Close box

Figure 1.4 *You can also click the close box to the current browser.*

Netscape has three types of principal windows: the Mail window, the News window, and Web browsers (sometimes called *browser windows*). You use browsers to view the pages available on the World Wide Web. Although you may only open one Mail or News window, you may open as many browsers as your computer's memory will permit. In this way, you can display several different pages at once. This is often useful if you want to follow a link on one page without losing track of the original source page.

Apart from viewing Web pages, browsers are also used to access FTP and Gopher sites.

Opening or closing a browser

Each time you launch Netscape, the program opens a new browser and connects to the specified home page. You can open a new browser at any time, in order to see new Web pages, without replacing the one in the current browser.

To open a browser:

Choose New Web Browser in the File menu **(Figure 1.1)**.

To close a browser:

Choose Close in the File menu **(Fig. 1.3)** or click the browser's close box **(Figure 1.4)**.

Choosing a home page

The first time you open a browser, Netscape jumps to the Web page that you have specified in the General Preferences dialog box. Although Netscape calls this your *home page,* don't confuse it with a Web site's home page. Instead, it is simply any page on the World Wide Web that you wish to jump to automatically upon opening Netscape. You may also set Netscape to open any HTML file on your hard disk.

Figure 1.5 *Choose General Preferences in the Options menu.*

To choose a home page:

1. Choose General Preferences in the Options menu **(Figure 1.5)**. The General Preferences dialog box appears.

2. Click the Appearance tab. The Appearance preferences appear **(Figure 1.6)**.

3. In the middle section, titled Startup, click Home Page Location.

4. Type the URL of the home page in the field directly below the Home Page Location option.

Figure 1.6 *Click Home Page Location under Browser starts with and then type the URL of the desired page.*

✔ Tips

■ Choose Blank Page under Browser starts with to have Netscape open new browsers with a blank page **(Figure 1.7)**.

■ You may save your bookmarks file or address book as an HTML file and then choose that file as your home page. For a home page that resides on your hard disk, type **file:///path/filename** in the Home Page Location field, where *path* is the location of the file on your hard disk and *filename* is its complete name.

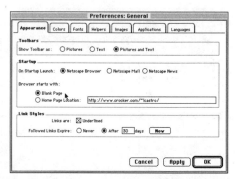

Figure 1.7 *To have Netscape open without connecting to a particular page, click Blank Page under Browser starts with. It doesn't matter what the Home Page Location text box contains.*

Figure 1.8 *The toolbar, location field, and directory buttons are showing by default.*

Figure 1.9 *Choose the appropriate command from the Options menu to hide (or reveal) the corresponding feature.*

Figure 1.10 *Once you hide the extra window items, you see more of the actual page.*

Figure 1.11 *Choose Save Options in the Options menu, so that the next time you open Netscape the same features are hidden (or revealed).*

Controlling a browser's appearance

Each browser can contain a toolbar full of buttons, a Location field, Directory buttons, and a status area **(Figure 1.8)**. You can choose to hide everything but the status area to save room on your screen and see more of your Web pages. You can also resize the window as necessary.

The toolbar contains a series of navigation and utility buttons. The Location field shows the URL address of the current Web page and can also be used to jump to different Web pages. The Directory buttons take you to particular pages on Netscape's Web site, or to other sites that Netscape has chosen for you.

To hide (or reveal) the toolbar, Location field, or Directory buttons:

Choose Show Toolbar, Show Location, or Show Directory Buttons in the Options menu to remove (or restore) the checkmark that is next to the command **(Fig. 1.9)**. The corresponding feature will disappear (or appear) **(Figure 1.10)**.

To save the browser's appearance:

Choose Save Options in the Options menu **(Figure 1.11)**. The next time you open Netscape, the browser will retain the size and features you have chosen.

Choosing fonts for the browser

In an attempt to keep Web pages as universal as possible, text only appears in one of two fonts, a proportional font like Times in which individual letters have different sizes, or a fixed width font like Courier in which all the characters are the same size.

You can choose which font (and size) you wish to use for displaying proportional text and which font (and size) should be used for displaying fixed width text.

To choose fonts for the browser:

1. Choose General Preferences in the Options menu **(Figure 1.12)**. The General Preferences dialog box appears.

2. Click the Fonts tab. The Fonts preferences are displayed.

3. Choose a font and size in the pop-up menus next to Use the Proportional Font to decide how most text in your Web pages (and messages) should be displayed **(Figure 1.13)**.

4. Choose a font and size in the pop-up menu next to Use the Fixed Font to decide how text in forms, block quotes and other special areas should be displayed.

5. Click OK to close the dialog box.

✔ Tip

■ You don't have to pick a fixed width font (like Courier) in the Fixed Width font pop-up menu. Pick any font you like.

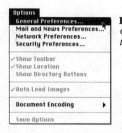

Figure 1.12 *Choose General Preferences in the Options menu.*

Figure 1.13 *Choose a font and size in the pop-up menus for each type of font. Click OK to save the changes.*

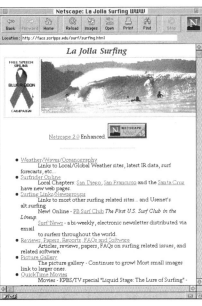

Figure 2.1 *There are over four million Web sites that you can surf to, each one different from the next.*

This is what you've been waiting for: actually getting to surf the World Wide Web. Although *surf* seems like a strange way to describe your activities as you sit in front of a computer, probably some distance from the beach, it does capture the idea of jumping from one Web page to another, perhaps reading and exploring as you go along, perhaps just enjoying the spray of information.

From its navigation buttons and keyboard shortcuts for getting from one place to another, to its clever new frames and history menu for remembering where you've been, Netscape makes surfing the Web as easy as it's ever been.

There are over four million Web sites (at press time), and several thousand more are added daily. You could spend your whole life wandering from page to page and never get to the end (although you might circle around to where you started). It's something like reading an encyclopedia: you'd learn a lot, but it would take you a long time.

In this section, we'll talk about how to get around on the Web with Netscape, assuming you already know where you want to go, or, on the other hand, that you don't really care where you end up. For more information on finding specific topics or pages, see Chapter 6, *Finding Stuff on the Web*.

What is a Web page?

So what are these things that you surf to? Actually, a Web page is nothing more than a text file written with special tags that format the contents, point to other pages, and insert images and sounds **(Fig. 2.2)**. The tags are called *HyperText Markup Language*, or HTML, and are quite easy to learn **(Figure 2.3)**.

With four million Web pages in existence, there is an incredible variety of designs and approaches, and of the kinds of information presented. It is probably safe to say that you can find a Web page about any topic you might choose to research—from Contra dancing to the Ethernet, from a subway map of major cities of the world to a database of every language spoken on each train.

Some Web pages are personal, designed by a single individual with information about themselves, their family and friends, perhaps their dog or cat, and their hobbies—as well as links to their favorite pages at other sites. Personal does not mean sloppy. As you'll find out, many of the best pages are created by people with no economic interest in the Web.

Other pages are strictly—or more subtly—commercial, created by (or for) a company in order to offer promotional information, technical support, upgrades, special tips, and other benefits to the public. Often, a commercial page's mission is simply to impress—with dazzling graphics, sounds or videos.

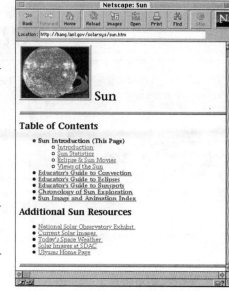

Figure 2.2 *This is a typical Web page, although perhaps more attractive and better organized than most. It was written by Calvin Hamilton, a private citizen like you or me, with the sole intention of sharing information and resources across the Internet.*

Figure 2.3 *This is the actual text that creates the page shown in Figure 2.2. The HTML codes are shown in less than and greater than signs "<>".*

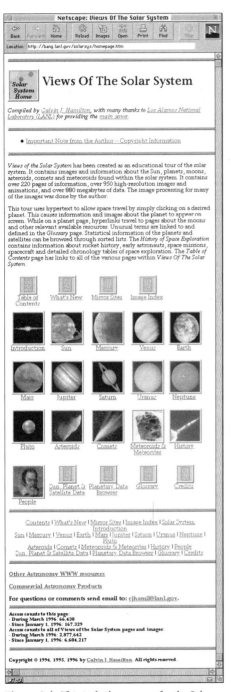

Figure 2.4 *This is the home page for the Solar System site. It contains an introduction, links to other pages at the site, and links to related sites.*

Sites, home pages, and servers

A Web *page* is a single text file written in HTML. A Web *site* is a collection of Web pages that belong to a single individual or company. Most Web sites have a special page, called a *home page,* that serves as a door to the rest of the site **(Figure 2.4)**. A home page generally has a banner explaining what the site contains—commercial sites usually include their company logo on the home page—as well as links to the other pages available at the site.

Beware: Although Netscape Communications knows exactly what a home page is, they've chosen to use the same term to denote the page that you jump to automatically upon launching the program *(see page 14)*. The page you choose may or may not be a *real* home page.

Web pages, including any graphics, sounds, videos or other external files, are stored on *servers*, dedicated computers that are connected to the Internet 24 hours a day—so that anyone, in any part of the world, can reach the Web page at any time.

Although you might think a server looks like something out of a movie—a huge hulking thing with those reel-to-reel tapes—any kind of computer can be a server, including Macs, PCs running Windows, and most often, Unix machines. The most important criterion for a server is not size or speed, but rather that it have a high-speed connection to the Internet so that it can handle the incoming requests for the Web sites it contains.

In addition to Web sites, servers can also contain FTP and Gopher sites, and manage e-mail and Usenet newsgroups.

Sites, home pages, and servers

Following links

A Web page's most distinguishing characteristic, and certainly the feature that has made Web surfing so popular and exciting, is its *links*. By clicking a link, you jump to another page, either at the same site or at a different site—which can be on the same server or, just as easily, at a site halfway around the world. You may also use links to jump to FTP and Gopher sites and to write e-mail.

Generally, new links—that is, the ones you have not yet visited—appear underlined and in blue (or in gray on monochrome monitors). Once you have followed a link to its destination, it will appear in purple so you can quickly distinguish new links from those you've already visited.

To follow a link:

1. In the current Web page, decide which link you wish to follow. Point to the link with the mouse. The link's URL appears in the status area at the bottom of the window **(Figure 2.5)**.

2. Click the link. Netscape takes you to the link's destination **(Figure 2.6)**.

✔ Tips

■ Open the link in a new window by clicking the link and choosing Open Link in New Window from the pop-up menu that appears.

■ You can always tell if a link is really a link by pointing at it with the mouse. If it is a link, the pointer will change into a pointing finger, and the link's destination will appear in the status area at the bottom of the browser.

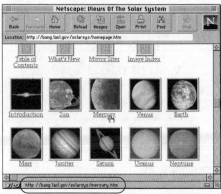

Figure 2.5 *When you place the pointer over a link (usually the blue, underlined items), the URL for the destination page appears at the bottom left corner of the browser.*

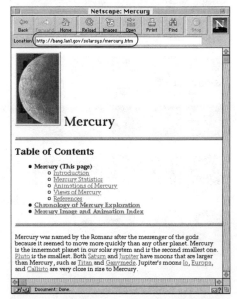

Figure 2.6 *When you click a link, Netscape loads the corresponding page. Notice how the URL in the Location field above matches the URL at the bottom left of Figure 2.5.*

Following links

Figure 2.7 *Choose General Preferences in the Options menu.*

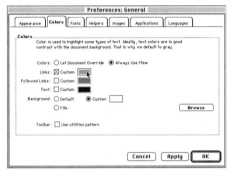

Figure 2.8 *Click the Colors tab and then click Custom next to Links or Followed Links and click in the color box.*

Figure 2.9 *Click on the Appearance tab and in the bottom section, click the Underlined option for Links are.*

Changing the appearance of links

Most pages show new links in blue and visited links in purple. However, a Web page designer can present her links in any colors she chooses—which can sometimes be confusing. Netscape also gives *you* the ability to view links in the colors that you prefer, and to show them underlined, or not.

To change the appearance of links:

1. Choose General Preferences in the Options menu **(Figure 2.7)**. The General Preferences box appears.

2. Click the Colors tab to show the preferences for Colors **(Figure 2.8)**.

3. Click the Custom box next to the type of links that you wish to change.

4. Click the corresponding color box. The Color picker appears.

5. Click on a new color in the Color picker and then click OK to save the changes. The new color appears to the right of the Custom box.

6. Repeat steps 3–5 for each kind of link.

7. To ensure that the links are always displayed with the colors you have chosen, click Always Use Mine for the Colors option.

8. Click the Appearance tab at the top of the General Preferences dialog box.

9. In the Link Styles section, check the Underlined box to display links with an underline; uncheck the box to remove underlining **(Figure 2.9)**.

10. Click OK to save the changes.

Jumping to a known page

If you already know the URL of the Web that you want to visit, the easiest way to get to the page is to be direct: tell Netscape.

To jump to a known page:

1. Choose Open Location in the File menu **(Fig. 2.10)** or click the Open button on the toolbar. The Open Location box appears **(Figure 2.11)**.

2. Type the desired URL in the text box, paying special attention to upper and lower case letters and punctuation.

3. Click Open to jump to the corresponding destination **(Figure 2.13)**.

✔ Tips

■ If a URL begins with *www (ftp, gopher)*, you don't need to type the protocol (**http://**, **ftp://**, or **gopher://**) at the beginning. Further, if a Web page address is in the form of *www.site.com*, you only need to type **site**.

■ You can also type a URL in the Location field just under the toolbar to jump to the corresponding page. As soon as you begin to type, the label changes to *Go To* **(Figure 2.12)**.

■ Choose New Web Browser in the File menu before going to a new page to open the page in a new browser.

■ You may jump to FTP and Gopher sites using these same techniques.

Figure 2.10 *Choose Open Location in the File menu.*

Figure 2.11 *In the Open Location dialog box that appears, type the URL of the page that you wish to jump to.*

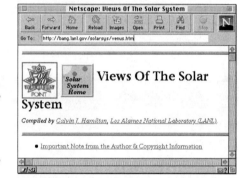

Figure 2.12 *In the Location field between the toolbar and the content area, type the URL of the desired page. As soon as you begin to type, the label changes from Location to Go To.*

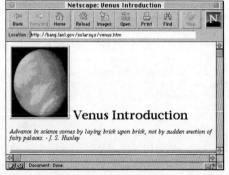

Figure 2.13 *Regardless of the method, Netscape loads the new page.*

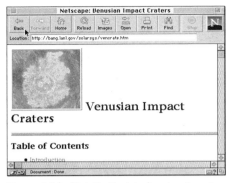

Figure 2.14 *Click the Back button to return to the last page you were browsing.*

Figure 2.15 *You can choose Back from the Go menu to get the same result.*

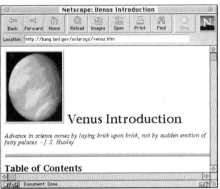

Figure 2.16 *Here, Netscape goes back to the Venus Introduction page, which as you can see in Figure 2.15 is the next page below the current page (Venusian Impact Craters) in the Go menu.*

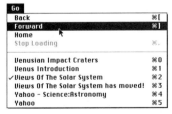

Figure 2.17 *Choose Forward in the Go menu to return to the page you just retreated from.*

Going back and forward

Perhaps one of the most difficult problems you'll have on the Web is following all of the links that interest you. Typically, you will find one Web page with several links that you want to follow. It's important to know how to get *back* to the page with the important links, once you've explored one or more of them.

To go back to the previous page:

Click the Back button on the toolbar **(Figure 2.14)** or choose Back in the Go menu **(Figure 2.15)**. Netscape will load the page that you visited immediately before jumping to the present page.

Going back means returning to the pages that brought you to the present page. *Going forward*, then, is turning around once again and following the same path that you did before. It's something like going back to where you came back from.

There are two conditions to going forward. First, you have to have gone back before you can go forward. Second, you must not have chosen a new link on an earlier page that brings you in a new direction. Since Netscape only remembers one path at a time, if you switch paths, all the most forward pages are forgotten.

To go forward:

Click the Forward button or choose Forward in the Go menu **(Figure 2.17)**. Netscape will bring you to the corresponding page.

Going further back or further ahead

As you wander around the Web, Netscape records the title and URL of each page that you visit and stores it in the Go menu. You can go back and revisit a page by choosing its title in the menu.

To go further back or further ahead:

Select the desired page from the Go menu **(Figure 2.18)**. Netscape jumps to the corresponding page **(Figure 2.19)**.

✔ Tips

■ Unfortunately, the Go menu only keeps track of the path of pages that has brought you to the current page. So if you backtrack (with the Back command or the Go menu) and then choose a link that leads you in a different direction, the references to the *later* pages will be lost.

■ One way to make sure the Go menu keeps track of *every* page you visit is to avoid using the Back and Forward commands and even the Go menu itself. If you need to go back to a page you have already visited, use the Open Location command instead.

■ To record a page's URL permanently, create a bookmark for it. For more details, see Chapter 7, *Bookmarks.*

■ Although the History window contains the same information as the Go menu, you may prefer to use it since it floats quietly on your screen— always at your fingertips. For more information, consult *Using the History window* on page 25.

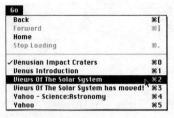

Figure 2.18 *You can choose any page in the Go menu to jump to that page.*

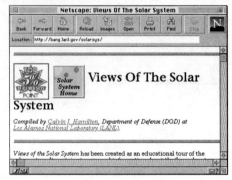

Figure 2.19 *A page that you select from the Go menu is often loaded faster than a brand new page since Netscape has already saved a copy of the page in its memory cache.*

Figure 2.20 *Choose History in the Window menu to display the History window on your screen.*

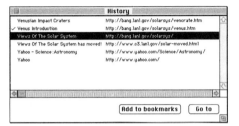

Figure 2.21 *The History window lets you see the pages that you have visited in the current session. You can jump to any page by double clicking it and add a bookmark by choosing the Add to bookmarks button.*

Using the History window

Netscape's History window keeps track of your travels on the Web. Each time you jump to a new page, the page's URL and title are added to the History window. However, the History window, like the Go menu, only keeps track of one path of pages at a time. That is, if you backtrack and then follow a new link in a new direction, all the pages after that page will be erased from the History window.

The principal advantage of the History window over the Go menu is that the History window can stay open on your screen, while the Go menu cannot.

To use the History window:

1. Choose History in the Window menu **(Figure 2.20)** to view the History window **(Figure 2.21)**.

2. Double click on a page to jump to that page. You can also click once and then click the Go to button.

3. Click on a page and then click Add to Bookmark to add a bookmark for that page to your Bookmarks window. For more information on bookmarks, see Chapter 7, *Bookmarks*.

4. To close the History window, simply click the close box.

✔ Tip

■ If you have the History window open as you begin to backtrack, a checkmark appears next to the current page in the History window, while the pages further ahead on the path remain visible.

Using the History window

Going to *your* home page

You can return to the home page that you specified in the General Preferences dialog box at any time with a simple click. For information on how to set your home page, consult *Choosing a home page* on page 14.

To go to your home page:

Click the Home button in the tool bar **(Figure 2.22)** or choose Home in the Go menu **(Figure 2.23)**. Netscape loads the home page specified in the Appearance tab of the General Preferences dialog box **(Figure 2.24)**.

✔ Tips

■ Remember, the Home button and Home menu commands bring you to *your* specified home page, not to the home page of the site that contains the page you are currently viewing (which would be much more useful, if you ask me).

■ Further, even if you have specified that Netscape *start* with a blank page, the program will still jump to the page specified in the General Preferences box when you use the Home button or command.

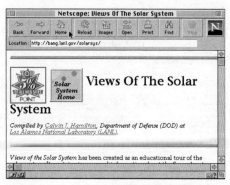

Figure 2.22 *Click the Home button to load the page specified in the General Preferences dialog box (not the site's home page).*

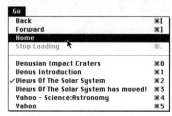

Figure 2.23 *You can also choose Home in the Go menu to load your home page.*

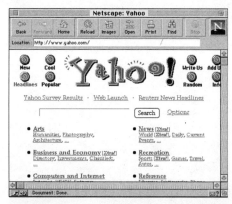

Figure 2.24 *This is my home page. A home page should either be a page that you consult often, or a page with a lot of links to other pages.*

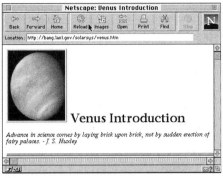

Figure 2.25 *Click the Reload button to have Netscape consult the server for any changes and update the page accordingly.*

Figure 2.26 *You can also choose Reload in the View menu to have Netscape update a page.*

Figure 2.27 *Hold down the Option key to get access to the Super Reload command.*

Reloading a page

When you jump to a page, Netscape automatically loads a copy of the page into its memory cache. The next time you jump to the page, instead of asking the server for the information (which might be rather slow, depending on the type of connection you have and the type of server that contains the page), it loads the page from memory.

However, if you suspect (or know) that the contents of the page have changed, if the page has not loaded completely, or if it has not loaded properly, you will want Netscape to load the page from the server and not from memory.

To reload a page:

Click the Reload button **(Figure 2.25)** or choose Reload in the View menu **(Figure 2.26)**. If the page's contents have changed, Netscape will get the new information from the server and will update the page accordingly. If the page has not changed, Netscape will reload it from memory.

✔ Tips

■ If you have trouble reloading a page that was changed in the last hour, the fault lies with Netscape and the "Daylight Savings Time" bug. Easiest solution? Update to a newer version of Netscape.

■ You can force a reload, regardless of the status of a page, by holding down the Option key and selecting Super Reload in the View menu **(Fig. 2.27)**.

Stopping a page from loading

As you get used to working with Netscape you'll get a feel for how fast it takes to get from one page to another and how long it takes average pages to load. There are three principal reasons why you might want to abort a jump to a page. First, you may simply have changed your mind, or made an errant click. Second, the page may be taking so long that you decide to go somewhere else. Finally, you may notice, as you watch the status bar, that Netscape takes an unusually long time to connect to the host. This is a good clue that either the server is busy or that the page is no longer located where you thought it was. Just abort the jump and move on.

To stop a page from loading:

1. Click the Stop button on the toolbar **(Figure 2.28)** or choose Stop Loading in the Go menu **(Figure 2.29)**. Netscape immediately stops trying to load the page and shows you what it's come up with so far, if anything. The word "Done" should appear in the status bar at the bottom left area of the window and the Netscape icon should stop shooting comets.

2. If part of the page has already loaded, and if you decide you really do want to continue loading the page, click the Reload button, or choose Reload in the View menu, to load the entire page.

✔ Tip

■ You can also press Command-Period to stop loading a page.

Figure 2.28 *You can stop loading a page at any time. Notice the progress information in the status area at the bottom left of the window and the half loaded image.*

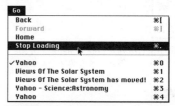

Figure 2.29 *You can also choose Stop Loading in the Go menu to break Netscape's link to the server.*

Figure 2.30 *This is another view of the page that I stopped loading in Figure 2.28. The image shown here never got a chance to begin loading and so the image placeholder icon is displayed in its place. You can load individual images by clicking them. For more information, consult Viewing images on the Web on page 29.*

Figure 2.31 *Choose Auto Load Images in the Options menu. A checkmark means the option is active. When the checkmark is absent, the images will not be loaded automatically.*

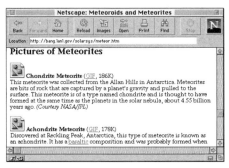

Figure 2.32 *With the Auto Load Images option off, the images are replaced with icons.*

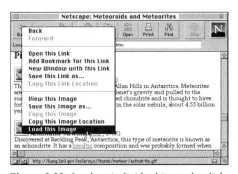

Figure 2.33 *Load an individual image by clicking it and choosing Load this Image in the menu.*

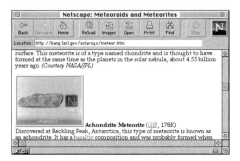

Figure 2.34 *The selected image is loaded.*

Viewing images on the Web

The two most common kinds of images that you'll find on the Web are GIF and JPEG images. Netscape can open both of these kinds of images automatically. However, since images tend to be large (and are always larger than text), they can take a long time to download and view. By default, Netscape automatically downloads all the JPEG and GIF images on the pages that you jump to. If you have a particularly slow connection, you may want to view only the text.

Deactivating automatic image download:

Choose Auto Load Images in the Options menu to remove the checkmark from the command **(Figure 2.31)**. The next time you jump to a page, the images will be displayed with placeholders **(Fig. 2.32)**.

When you have the Auto Load Images command deactivated, you can choose to load all the images in a particular page, or to load one or more individual images.

To load all the images on a page:

Choose Load Images in the View menu. The placeholders are replaced by the corresponding images. You can also click the Load Images button on the toolbar.

To load a particular image:

Click the desired image and choose Load this Image in the pop-up menu **(Figure 2.33)**. Netscape displays the corresponding image **(Figure 2.34)**.

Helper applications

Currently, Netscape can't view all kinds of files internally. Although this will change as more features are added, right now you can count on Netscape only for text, and certain kinds of images, especially GIF and JPEG. For other kinds of files, like sounds or movies, it calls up another application—usually one that is small and fast and dedicated to opening and viewing one particular kind of file—to do the job.

The small, dedicated applications used for opening and viewing multimedia files on the Web are called "helper applications" and can often be downloaded for free via FTP. There are helper apps (as they're affectionately known) for decompressing files, viewing PostScript files, viewing video and images, listening to sounds and more.

Common helper apps for Macintosh:

Type	Name
Graphics	JPEGView
	GraphicConverter
Sound	SoundMachine
	RealAudio
Video	Sparkle
	FastPlayer
PDF	Amber

You can find helper apps to download on many pages all over the Web. For more help, consult Chapter 6, *Finding Stuff on the Web.*

Figure 2.35 *If you click a link to a multimedia file that Netscape can't open on its own, it will launch a helper application to deal with the file.*

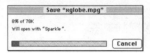

Figure 2.36 *Netscape automatically downloads the files that it can't read on its own.*

Figure 2.37 *Once the file has finished downloading, Netscape launches the helper application which opens the file and displays it. This is a movie of the Earth rotating.*

Figure 2.38 *Choose General Preferences in the Options menu.*

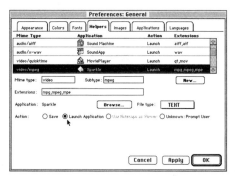

Figure 2.39 *Choose the desired file type in the list, click Launch Application and then click Browse.*

Figure 2.40 *Find the helper application on your hard disk and click Open.*

Setting up helper apps

Once you've downloaded the helper applications on your hard disk, you must tell Netscape where they can be found and which ones should be used with which files.

To set up helper apps:

1. Choose General Preferences in the Options menu **(Figure 2.38)**. The General Preferences box appears.

2. Click the Helpers tab to view the Helpers apps preferences.

3. Select the file type that you wish to associate with a particular helper application **(Figure 2.39)**.

4. Next to Action, choose Launch Application.

5. Click Browse. A dialog box appears in which you can indicate the name and location of the helper application.

6. Locate the helper app and click Open **(Figure 2.40)**.

7. Repeat steps 3–6 for each helper app you wish to assign to a particular kind of file.

✔ Tip

■ Some installers complete this process for you. Check the helper app's documentation to be sure.

Setting up helper apps

When no helper app is available

There may be many kinds of files that you never—or rarely—encounter and for which you don't have the corresponding helper application. In this case, you can have Netscape either save the file to disk or ask you what program to use to open the file.

To set options when no helper app is available:

1. Choose General Preferences in the Options menu **(Figure 2.41)**.

2. Click the Helpers tab to view the Helpers apps preferences.

3. Select the file type that you want to set options for **(Figure 2.42)**.

4. Choose Save if you want Netscape to automatically save the file in your hard disk. Choose Unknown: Prompt User to have Netscape alert you each time it encounters a file it doesn't know what to do with.

5. Click OK to save the changes.

✔ Tips

■ You might want to use the Save option for files from another platform that you don't want to open on the present computer.

■ Netscape automatically views text files in the browser. To automatically save text files, select the *text/plain* file type and then choose Save. Don't choose Save for *text/html* files, or you won't be able to view Web pages.

Figure 2.41 *Choose General Preferences in the Options menu.*

Figure 2.42 *Select the desired file type and then click either Save or Unknown: Prompt User in the Action section.*

Frames

Figure 3.1 *A frame is a regular page with its own URL (like the one above) that is fit into a frameset like the one shown in Figure 3.2.*

Figure 3.2 *A frameset is a page that is divided into individual frames, each of which displays the information from its own URL.*

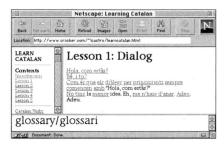

Figure 3.3 *Oftentimes when you click a link in one frame, the corresponding URL is shown in one of the other frames, while all the remaining frames stay constant.*

With version 2, Netscape introduced frames, an ingenious feature that divides each window into individual panes that each hold their own URL. Frames make it easy to hold on to one page (say, that contains a series of links, like a table of contents) while viewing a whole series of others (where the links lead). Navigating such sites can be confusing; this chapter should make it easier to get around.

Frames and framesets

A *frame* is nothing more than a regular Web page that has been shoe-horned into a smaller area within another Web page, called a *frameset*. The frameset contains information about the size of the frames within it, including their sizes, names, scrolling qualities, and URLs **(Figure 3.2)**.

When you click on a link inside a frame, one of two things can happen. If the link is to a page at the same site, it will usually appear inside the currently open frameset, replacing the contents of one of the existing frames. The other frames remain unchanged so that you can still see the information that they contain **(Fig. 3.3)**.

If the link is to a page at a different site, the page will usually open up in a new window. If it doesn't and you want it to, consult *Opening a frame in a new window* on page 35 for more details.

Perhaps the most important thing to remember is that you, the Web surfer, cannot create or add frames to an existing page. You can only navigate the frames that are already there.

Following a link in a frame

Following a link on a page with frames is practically identical to following links on regular pages *(see page 20)*: simply click and go. The difference is in where the result will be displayed. When you click on a link in a frameset, the link is usually opened in one of the frames, while the other frames remain unchanged.

To follow a link in a frame:

1. Place the pointer over the link that you wish to jump to **(Figure 3.5)**. You may have to scroll around in the frame to make the link visible.

2. Click the link. Netscape brings you to the link's destination **(Figure 3.6)**. Many times, the page will be displayed inside one of the frames in the current frameset.

✔ Tips

■ You can't open a link in a specific frame unless the designer has allowed for it, but you can open the link in a new window *(see page 35)*.

■ Usually, a frameset contains a narrow frame with links, a central frame where those links are displayed and sometimes a static frame that contains a logo or toolbar.

■ You can often resize frames to better suit your needs. For more information, consult *Resizing and scrolling around a frame* on page 36.

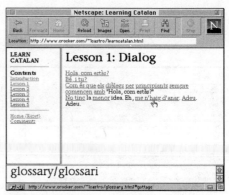

Figure 3.5 *Follow the link in one of the frames in the usual way, by positioning the cursor over the link until it turns into a hand. Then click the mouse.*

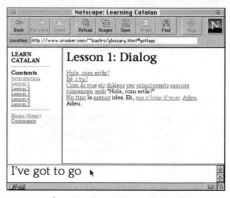

Figure 3.6 *In this example, the corresponding URL is displayed in the bottom frame. The other frames remain unchanged.*

Figure 3.7 *Navigate to a page that has a link to the desired frame.*

Figure 3.8 *Place the pointer over the link and hold down the mouse button until the pop-up menu appears. Choose New Window with this Link in the pop-up menu.*

Figure 3.9 *The selected link is opened in a new browser.*

Opening a frame in a new window

Often, links are *targeted* to particular frames. That means that when you click the link, the corresponding URL appears within a specific frame. If the frame is too small or too unwieldy, you may wish to open the link in a separate, independent window.

To open a frame in a new window:

1. Navigate to a page that has a link to the desired frame **(Figure 3.7)**.

2. Place the pointer over the link and hold down the mouse button until the pop-up menu appears **(Figure 3.8)**.

3. Choose New Window with this Link in the pop-up menu. The link (that was usually displayed in a frame) is displayed in a new browser **(Figure 3.9)**.

✔ Tip

■ Sloppy Web page designers sometimes make links to external sites appear inside a frame. If the external site happens to have its own frames, the whole frameset will be stuffed into the frame on the original page. The best thing to do is go back *(see page 37)* and then open the link in a new window.

Resizing and scrolling around a frame

Depending on how the Web page designer has written the HTML for the frameset, a frame can either have a fixed size (in pixels), a relative size (that depends on the size of the whole browser), or be adjustable by the user.

In my opinion, since there is no way to foresee what size browser a user will have, designers should always make frames adjustable. Unfortunately, not all Web page designers agree.

To resize a frame:

1. Place the pointer over one of the borders of the frame **(Figure 3.10)**. If it changes into a double pointed arrow, you can change the size of the frame.

2. Drag the border to the desired new position **(Figure 3.11)**.

Similarly, a designer can create a frameset so that a frame has scroll bars all the time, none of the time, or only when necessary.

To scroll around a frame:

1. If the scroll bars are visible, click on the up or down arrows to see more information at the top or bottom of the frame, respectively. Drag the scroll box to move more quickly. Click in the gray area to move one frame area at a time **(Figure 3.12)**.

2. Or, select the frame (by clicking in it) and use the arrow keys to move around the frame.

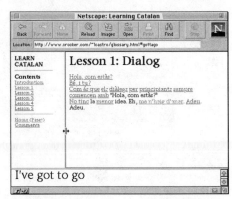

Figure 3.10 *Place the cursor between the frames. When it changes to a double-pointed arrow, drag it to resize the frames.*

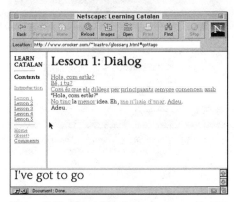

Figure 3.11 *The right column is narrower now.*

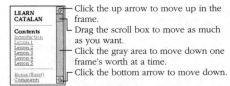

Figure 3.12 *The scroll bars (if they're visible) let you move around the frame to see additional information.*

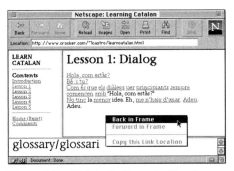

Figure 3.13 *Click in the frame, holding down the mouse button until the pop-up menu appears. Choose Back in Frame (or Forward in Frame) from the pop-up menu.*

Figure 3.14 *The previous contents of the selected frame are shown. Notice that the other frames remain unchanged.*

Going backward or forward in a frame

The Back and Forward buttons on the toolbar refer to pages, not to frames. Remember that a set of frames is contained in a single page (called a *frameset*). If you click the Back or Forward button, you'll go back or forward *a whole page*, and in particular, to the page you were browsing before you jumped to the frameset page. If you want to go back or forward a frame, you have to use the pop-up menu.

To go backward or forward in a frame:

1. Place the pointer inside the frame that you want to go back or forward in, anywhere except over a link **(Figure 3.13)**.

2. Press the right mouse button to display the pop-up menu.

3. Choose Back in Frame or Forward in Frame in the pop-up menu. Netscape shows the appropriate information in the selected frame **(Figure 3.14)**.

✔ Tip

■ You can only go backward or forward in a frame if you've actually shown more than one URL in that frame. If not, the Back in Frame (or Forward in Frame) commands in the pop-up menu will be grayed out.

Going backward or forward in a frame

Transferring Files

In order to transfer files from one computer to another, for example, from a server in New Jersey to your house, the two computers need to speak to each other the same way—with the same *protocol*. Before the Web, the most common protocols for downloading files were FTP (which stands for *file transfer protocol*) and Gopher. And even though today it's quite simple to download files from a Web page, most servers continue to offer files through the two older systems.

Netscape allows you to access FTP or Gopher servers in much the same way as you would regular Web servers by displaying their contents as a series of hierarchical folders.

FTP and Gopher servers do not have links to other sites, and generally they don't include explanatory text. They are dedicated to file transfer. Some sites are open to the public, while others are restricted to particular users.

To transfer files to another person or company via e-mail, consult *Attaching files to a message* on page 120.

Accessing an FTP site

Many servers offer either anonymous or private FTP. Universities, Internet service providers, and computer manufacturers typically offer anonymous FTP access to their files, which may be doctoral dissertations, Web software or program updates, respectively, among many other possibilities. In addition, you may have access to a private FTP site at your own server.

To access an FTP site:

1. Choose Open Location in the File menu or click the Open button on the toolbar **(Figure 4.1)**. The Open Location dialog box appears.

2. For an anonymous FTP site, type **ftp.site** where *ftp.site* is the URL address of the desired FTP site **(Figure 4.2)**. To access a private FTP site, you'll have to type **ftp://user name:password@ftp.site**.

3. Click Open. Netscape contacts the FTP server and displays the contents of the FTP site **(Figure 4.3)**.

✔ Tips

■ You can also type the FTP address in the Location text box under the toolbar, if it is showing *(see page 15)*.

■ If the anonymous FTP address begins with the word *ftp*, you don't need to type the initial **ftp://**; Netscape will add it automatically **(Figure 4.4)**.

■ Anonymous FTP sites often limit the number of people that can connect at a time. If you get an error message, try again later. According to Internet etiquette, you shouldn't access a university site during business hours.

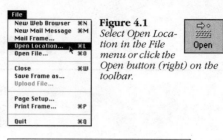

Figure 4.1
Select Open Location in the File menu or click the Open button (right) on the toolbar.

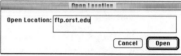

Figure 4.2 *Type the FTP address in the Open Location dialog box and click Open.*

Figure 4.3 *The FTP site is displayed in the browser. Click on a folder to see its contents. Click on a file to download it.*

Figure 4.4 *You only have to type* ftp:// *at the beginning of the URL if the FTP address itself does not begin with the letters* ftp.

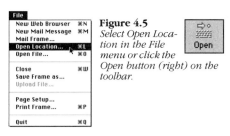

Figure 4.5
Select Open Location in the File menu or click the Open button (right) on the toolbar.

Figure 4.6 *Type the URL of the desired Gopher site in the Open Location dialog box.*

Figure 4.7 *The Gopher site is displayed. Click a folder to access its contents. Click a text file to display it.*

Figure 4.8 *When you click a text document, it is displayed in the browser.*

Accessing a Gopher site

The Gopher protocol, supported by many university sites, lets you search databases and retrieve files. Although there continues to be wide support for Gopher, it has been generally supplanted by the Web.

To access a Gopher site:

1. Choose Open Location in the File menu or click the Open button on the toolbar **(Figure 4.5)**. The Open Location dialog box appears.

2. Type **gopher.site** where *gopher.site* is the URL address of the desired Gopher site **(Figure 4.6)**.

3. Click Open. Netscape contacts the Gopher server and displays the available files on screen **(Figure 4.7)**.

4. Click on a folder to see its contents. Click on a text file to display it **(Figure 4.8)**.

✔ Tips

■ If the Gopher address begins with the word *gopher*, you don't need to type the initial **gopher://**; Netscape will add it automatically.

■ You can also type the Gopher address in the Location bar in the main Netscape window, if it is showing *(see page 15)*.

Accessing a Gopher site

Downloading files

Once you have accessed the desired FTP, Gopher, or Web site, actually downloading a file is only a click away.

To download a file:

1. Access the desired site.

2. Click on the appropriate folders until you find the file you wish to download **(Figure 4.9)**.

3. Click the desired file. Netscape may ask you what to do with the file. Click Save File to save it to your hard disk.

4. In the Save As dialog box that appears, choose the directory in which to save the file and click Save **(Figure 4.10)**.

5. Netscape initiates the transfer and shows the Save file dialog box which indicates the size of the file and how long it will take to download **(Figure 4.11)**.

6. If you change your mind about downloading the file, click the Cancel button in the Save file dialog box.

✔ Tips

■ Netscape automatically displays text files in the browser instead of saving them. To save a text file, click it and choose Save this Link as in the pop-up menu. For more information, consult *Saving a page without jumping to it* on page 47.

■ You can set up Netscape so that it uncompresses certain kinds of files automatically. For more information, consult *Setting up helper apps* on page 31.

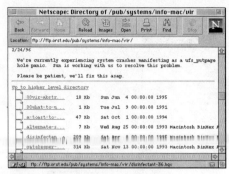

Figure 4.9 *Find the file that you wish to download from an FTP or Gopher site, or from a Web page. You may have to wade through several layers of folders. Click the file to download it.*

Figure 4.10 *Netscape shows you the Save As dialog box. Give the file a name, choose a location and click Save.*

Figure 4.11 *The Save file dialog box shows how large the file is and how long it will take to download. You can click Cancel to abort the download at any time.*

Figure 4.12 *Navigate to the FTP site where you want to upload the file.*

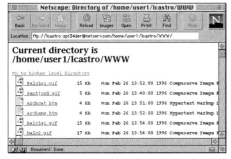

Figure 4.13 *Choose and open the folder (WWW, in this case) in which you wish to save the file.*

Figure 4.14 *Choose Upload File in the File menu.*

Figure 4.15 *In the Open dialog box that appears, select the file on your hard disk that you wish to upload. Click Open.*

Uploading a file with FTP

Although you can download a file from an FTP, Gopher, or Web site, you can usually only upload a file to an FTP site. You might want to upload a Web page that you've created to your Internet service provider's server so that other users can have access to it. Or a software manufacturer might ask you to upload a file that lists your system extensions so that they can help you with a bombing program.

To upload a file with FTP:

1. Access the FTP site and navigate to the desired folder in which you wish to upload the file **(Figure 4.12 and Figure 4.13)**.

2. Choose Upload file in the File menu **(Figure 4.14)**.

3. In the dialog box that appears—that displays the contents of your hard disk—choose the desired file and click Open **(Figure 4.15)**. The file is transferred to the FTP site.

4. If you change your mind about uploading the file, click the Cancel button in the File Upload dialog box or the Stop button on the toolbar.

✔ Tips

■ You may continue using Netscape while you are uploading a file. Of course, it won't be as fast as if it were dedicated to the one task.

■ Be careful when you upload files. Once you've uploaded them, you can't change their location with Netscape. Of course, you can use a dedicated FTP client like Fetch to move files around on the FTP server.

Uploading a file with FTP

Uploading multiple files

You can upload several files at once to an FTP site using drag and drop. To do so, you drag files from the desktop directly to the Netscape browser which you've previously opened to your FTP site.

To upload multiple files:

1. Connect to your FTP site *(see page 40)* and navigate to the desired destination directory **(Figure 4.16)**.

2. Select the desired files on the desktop **(Figure 4.17)**.

3. Drag the files to the Netscape browser showing the FTP site **(Figure 4.18)**.

4. Click the Netscape browser to make it active. An alert appears asking if you wish to upload the dragged files to the FTP site **(Figure 4.19)**.

5. Click OK in the alert. The files are uploaded.

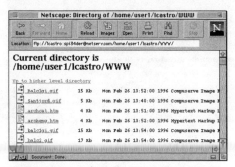

Figure 4.16 *Connect to the FTP site and navigate to the desired destination directory.*

Figure 4.17 *In the Finder, select the files that you wish to upload.*

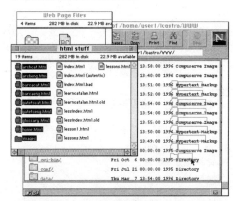

Figure 4.18 *Drag the files to the Netscape window, inactive but visible behind the Finder.*

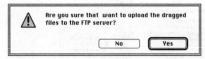

Figure 4.19 *When you click on the Netscape window, this alert appears. Click Yes to upload the files.*

Uploading multiple files

Saving and Printing

As you surf, you may find images and text that you would like to save. Although much of the material on the Web is copyrighted, you are allowed to save files for your own use—for example, to read a page or view an image after you have disconnected from your online service.

The images that you find on Web pages can only be saved in their original format. You will have to use a separate program like GraphicConverter or Adobe Photoshop to convert them to other formats.

If you find a particularly interesting page and you want to keep a copy of it, or share it with someone who's (gasp) not on the Web, you can print out a copy.

Saving a Web page

Netscape can save a Web page with or without its HTML tags. To open the file with a word processor and work with the data in some way, you should save the page *without* HTML tags—Netscape calls this "Text" format.

To read the page with Netscape once you've disconnected from your online service, or to study other peoples' HTML, you should save the file *with* HTML tags—Netscape calls this "Source" format.

To save a Web page:

1. Jump to the desired page **(Fig. 5.1)**.

2. Choose Save As in the File menu **(Fig. 5.2)**. The Save As box appears.

3. In the Format submenu at the bottom of the dialog box **(Figure 5.3)**, choose Source to save the page with HTML tags, or Text to save the page without HTML tags.

4. If you save the file with HTML tags, be sure to add the extension .html to the file name so that all browsers on all platforms can recognize the file.

5. Give the file a name and click OK. A progress bar indicates how long it will take **(Figure 5.4)**.

✔ Tips

■ Don't be confused by Netscape's use of *Text* and *Source*. All Web pages— even those saved with HTML tags in Source format—are text files.

■ Images are not downloaded when you save a page. To save images, see page 48.

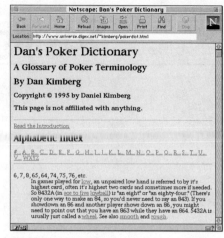

Figure 5.1 *First, navigate to the page that you want to save.*

Figure 5.2 *Choose Save As in the File menu.*

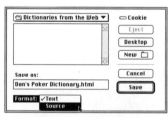

Figure 5.3 *Choose either Source or Text in the pop-up menu, give the file a name (or use the existing one) and then click Save.*

Figure 5.4 *A progress bar will appear telling you how long it will take to save the file to disk.*

Figure 5.5 *First, navigate to a page that contains a link to the page you want to save. Place the pointer over the link.*

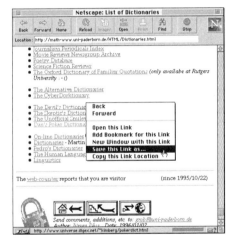

Figure 5.6 *Press down the mouse button until the pop-up menu appears and then choose Save this Link as.*

Figure 5.7 *Choose either Source or Text in the pop-up menu, give the file a name (or use the existing one) and then click OK.*

Saving a page without jumping to it

You can save a Web page without even navigating to it. This is convenient when you are on a page with several links to other interesting looking pages, since you can save each of the other pages without leaving the main page that has the links.

To save a page without jumping to it:

1. Jump to a page that contains a link to the page you wish to save **(Fig. 5.5)**.

2. Click the link and choose Save this Link as in the menu **(Figure 5.6)**.

3. In the Format submenu at the bottom of the Save As box that appears, choose Source to save the page with HTML tags, or Text to save the page without HTML tags **(Figure 5.7)**.

4. If you save the file with HTML tags, be sure to add the extension .html to the file name so that all browsers on all platforms can recognize the file.

5. Change the file name if desired and click OK.

✔ Tips

■ Hold down the Option key and click a link to save the corresponding page without using the pop-up menu.

■ When you save a Web page with the Save as command *(see page 46)*, the default file name is the title of the Web page. When you save a *link* to a page, the default file name is the original file name. Use the original file names if you want the internal links between a set of related pages to work offline.

Saving an image

Inline images are not downloaded automatically when you save a Web page. Instead, you must save each image separately.

External images, on the other hand, are usually downloaded to your hard disk automatically when you view them. For more information, consult *Helper applications* on page 68.

To save an inline image:

1. Navigate to the page that contains the image.

2. Click the image and choose Save this Image as in the pop-up menu **(Figure 5.8)**. The Save As dialog box appears **(Figure 5.9)**.

3. Click OK to save the image with the name and extension given. The Saving Location dialog box shows you how long the download will take to finish **(Figure 5.10)**.

✔ Tips

■ Although you can change the extension of an image file when you save it, this will *not* magically change its format. To change an image's format, you need to use a program like GraphicConverter or Photoshop.

■ You can also save an image by holding down the Option key and clicking the image with the mouse button.

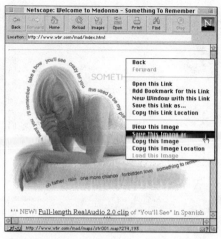

Figure 5.8 *To save an inline image, click on the image and hold down the mouse button until the pop-up menu appears. Then choose Save this Image as to save the image.*

Figure 5.9 *In the Save image dialog box, choose a file name (or use the existing one) and click Save.*

Figure 5.10 *A progress bar appears to show you how long it will take to download the image. You may continue browsing by clicking the main window.*

Figure 5.11 *Place the pointer over the desired image (and who has a more carefully designed image than Madonna?) and hold down the mouse button until the pop-up menu appears. Then choose Copy this image from the menu.*

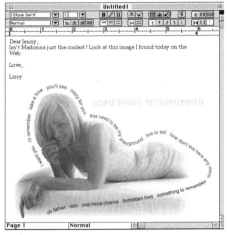

Figure 5.12 *Then paste the image into the desired document with the Paste command.*

Copying an image

If you want to copy a single inline image, just selecting it with the mouse won't be enough.

To copy a single inline image:

1. Place the cursor over the desired image and press the mouse button until the pop-up menu appears.

2. Select Copy this Image in the pop-up menu **(Figure 5.11)**. The image is copied to the clipboard.

3. Switch to the application and document into which you wish to paste the copied image.

4. Choose Paste in the Edit menu of that application. The image is pasted in the desired document **(Figure 5.12)**.

✔ **Tip**

■ Many images on the Web are copyrighted. It is against the law to use copyrighted images without permission of the author. On the other hand, it's probably OK to use them in personal documents like the one in Figure 5.12.

Copying and pasting parts of a page

There is no law that says you must save an entire page when you are only interested in one portion of it. In addition, copying the page as described below is a fast and easy way to transfer information to other files in other applications.

To copy and paste part of a page:

1. With the mouse, select the part of the page that you wish to copy **(Figure 5.13)**.

2. Choose Copy in the Edit menu or press Command-C **(Figure 5.14)**.

3. Place the cursor where you want to paste the material (perhaps in an e-mail note, in another application, or wherever).

4. Choose Paste in the Edit menu or press Command-V. The text is pasted into the current window **(Fig. 5.15)**.

✔ Tips

■ HTML tags and images cannot be copied using this technique. To save a page with HTML tags, consult *Saving a Web page* on page 46. To copy images, consult *Saving an image* on page 48.

■ You may not paste anything into an existing Web page in the Netscape browser. Of course, you may open a Web page (saved with HTML tags) with a word processor and then paste parts of other pages into it there.

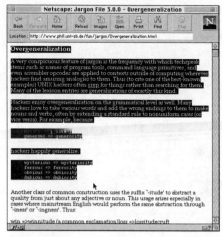

Figure 5.13 *Select (with the mouse) the part of the page that you wish to copy.*

Figure 5.14 *Choose Copy in the Edit menu.*

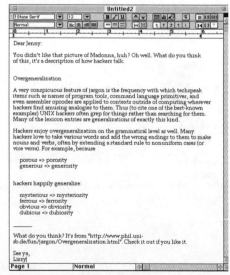

Figure 5.15 *Here I've pasted the copied material into a letter (in Microsoft Word).*

Figure 5.16 *To open a saved file, choose Open File in Netscape's File menu.*

Figure 5.17 *In the Open dialog box, choose the desired file and click Open.*

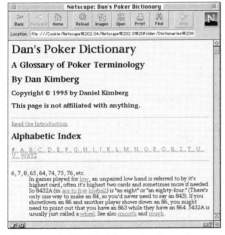

Figure 5.18 *The file (if saved as Source) appears exactly as it did originally.*

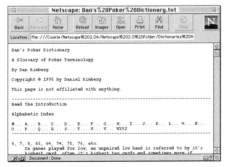

Figure 5.19 *If the file was saved as Text, it appears without formatting or links.*

Reading a saved page offline

If you've found an interesting but long page that you would like to read without hearing the connect-time clock ticking anxiously at your back, you can save the page, disconnect from your online service, and then open the page to read.

To read a saved page offline:

1. Save the page *with HTML tags* using the techniques described on page 46 or page 47.

2. Without quitting Netscape, disconnect from your online service.

3. From Netscape's File menu, choose Open File **(Figure 5.16)**. The Open dialog box appears.

4. Choose the file you saved in step 1 and click Open **(Fig. 5.17)**. The page will appear in the Netscape browser **(Figure 5.18)**.

5. Read at your leisure.

✔ Tips

■ If you are saving several related pages for later reading, make sure to save them with their original names *(see page 47)*.

■ You can also view saved GIF or JPEG images offline. Simply choose the image in step 4 above. The image appears by itself in the browser.

■ If you saved the page in Text format, it appears quite differently in the browser—without formatting, images or links **(Figure 5.19)**.

Reading a saved page offline

Printing a page

You may want to create a hard copy of one of the pages that you find on the Web for future reference. Netscape automatically resizes the information on the Web page to fit on the printed page.

To print a page:

1. Navigate to the page that you wish to print **(Figure 5.20)**.

2. Choose Print in the File menu or click the Print button on the toolbar **(Figure 5.21)**. The standard Print dialog box appears.

3. If desired, change the printing options.

4. Click Print **(Figure 5.22)**. The page will be printed.

✔ Tips

■ Printing an e-mail message, news posting or page that you are editing is practically identical to printing a Web page. Simply view the desired item and choose Print from the File menu.

■ Print an individual frame by clicking in the frame before choosing Print Frame in the File menu.

■ For more printer options, consult *Setting up printing options* on page 53.

Figure 5.20 *Navigate to the page (frame, message, posting) that you want to print.*

Figure 5.21 *Choose Print in the File menu.*

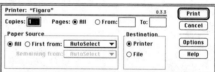

Figure 5.22 *In the standard Print dialog box, choose the desired options and then click Print.*

Printing a page

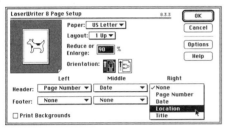

Figure 5.23 *Choose Page Setup in the File menu.*

Figure 5.24 *Choose the options in the pop-up menus next to, and below, the area where you want the item to be printed.*

Setting up printing options

When you print a document, you can choose to include the page number, date, location of the page (i.e., its URL), or title in the header or footer of each printed page. You can also choose to print a page's background.

To set the printing options:

1. Choose Page Setup in the File menu **(Figure 5.23)**. The Page Setup dialog box appears **(Figure 5.24)**.

2. In the Header section, select the item (Page Number, Date, Location or Title) in the pop-up menu, under the desired area where you want that item to be printed in the header.

3. Repeat step 2 for the Footer section.

4. Click Print Backgrounds if you want to include colorful or image-based backgrounds when you print a Web page. Leave the option unchecked to print pages with a white background.

5. Click OK to save the options.

✔ Tip

■ The options in the Page Setup dialog box affect all the pages you print from that moment onwards, not just the current document.

Setting up printing options

Finding Stuff on the Web

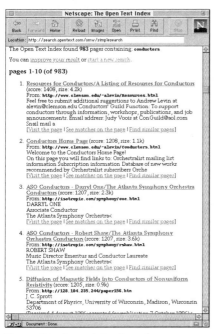

Figure 6.1 *A search for the rather vague con-ductors finds 983 pages, some of which, like number 5, are about physics, not musicians.*

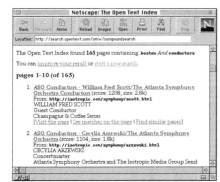

Figure 6.2 *A search for* Boston *and* conduc-tors, *on the other hand, results in only 165 matches.*

With millions of Web pages, fourteen thousand newsgroups, and countless e-mail users, it is sometimes a challenge to find the information that you're looking for. There are many companies that offer Internet search services in exchange for a glance at their advertisers' promotions.

There are services that search Web pages, services that search newsgroups, services that search for e-mail addresses and even services that catalog shareware. You sim-ply jump to the service that is most likely to have the information you need.

Tips for using search services

First, when typing search or keywords, try to be as specific as possible without being too specific. That is, if you're looking for Web pages about Seiji Ozawa, instead of typing *conductors*, which is very general, you might try *Boston conductors* (since he is the conductor of the Boston Symphony). Or, instead of typing *Seiji Ozawa*, which is very specific, try just *Ozawa*.

Second—and this may sound obvious—be careful with spelling. If you don't spell the keywords right, the search service won't be able to find the desired page. If the word has an alternate spelling (which is often the case with words from other languages— Gorbachev or Gorbachov?) or if it is mis-spelled on the page itself, you can use the boolean operator OR to search for several spellings simultaneously.

Tips for using search services

Finding Web pages by subject

One of the best known Web page search indexes is Yahoo!. Yahoo! sorts its Web index by topic, and creates a kind of Table of Contents for the Web. If you want to see several pages about the same or related general topics, or if you just want a place to start surfing, Yahoo! is a good place to begin.

To use Yahoo! to find Web pages by topic:

1. Choose Open Location in the File menu or click the Open button on the toolbar **(Figure 6.3)**. The Open Location dialog box appears **(Figure 6.4)**.

2. Type **yahoo** in the text box and click Open. Netscape displays the Yahoo! home page **(Figure 6.5)**. Each main topic is divided into clickable subtopics.

3. Click any topic or subtopic of interest. Yahoo! displays a set of related links **(Figure 6.6)**. The links may be divided into indices (lists of related links), subtopics (which when clicked on reveal a list of links to pages about the subtopic) or Web pages (that fit the general topic but none of the subtopics listed).

4. Click the desired link **(Figure 6.8)**. The page is displayed.

✔ Tip

■ You can also search for keywords through Yahoo! by entering the words in the text box and clicking Search. However, there are other services that are better at straight word searches.

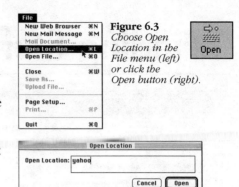

Figure 6.3
Choose Open Location in the File menu (left) or click the Open button (right).

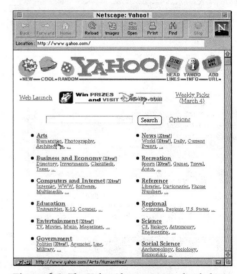

Figure 6.4 *Type Yahoo's URL in the Open Location dialog box.*

Figure 6.5 *The Yahoo! home page is divided into categories and subcategories, according to topic, all of which contain links to related articles.*

Finding Web pages by subject

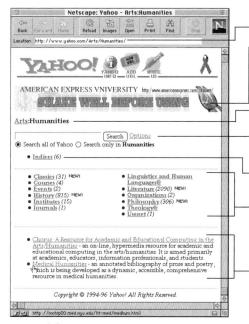

Yahoo's address is displayed in the Location text box.

Advertisements are sprinkled liberally throughout the Yahoo! site. This is how Yahoo! makes money, but you don't have to pay attention.

Yahoo! always lists the path that you have taken. You can click on the links to the earlier pages to go back (up) in the hierarchy of categories.

You can also choose to search for a keyword, either in the entire Yahoo! index, or just in the pages that are in the currently selected category.

The Indices are pages that contain a collection of links to the main topic (Humanities, in this case).

Yahoo! divides all the articles into subcategories. The number after each category indicates how many articles it contains. An @ symbol means that the subcategory is further divided into smaller subcategories.

The articles that are general enough to be related to the main category (Humanities) but that don't fit into any subcategories, are listed at the bottom of the page.

Figure 6.6 *A click on Humanities brings up this page of related links, divided into subcategories.*

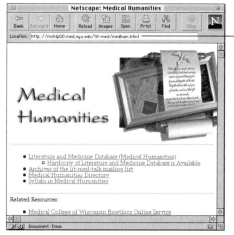

The selected page is not part of the Yahoo! site; Yahoo! just helped you find it. This page is actually from New York University's Medical School.

Figure 6.7 *A click on a link in Figure 6.6 brings you to the corresponding article out on the Web. You are not longer at the Yahoo! site.*

Finding Web pages by subject

Searching for Web pages by keyword

There are two or three good search services that have indexed as much of the Web as they can find—by sending out automatic robots called *spiders* that go from server to server looking at all the Web pages and recording their addresses, titles and sometimes even their contents. Perhaps the best service I've found is Open Text, that claims to contain more than 8 billion words in its index.

To search for Web pages by keyword with Open Text:

1. Choose Open Location or click the Open button on the toolbar. The Open Location dialog box appears.

2. Type **www.opentext.com/omw/f-omw.html** (yes, even that dash) in the text box and click Open **(Figure 6.8)**. Netscape displays the Open Text home page.

3. Type a word or phrase in the first box **(Figure 6.9)**.

4. If desired, choose where you wish Open Text to search (anywhere, summary, title, first heading, web location) in the pop-up menu.

5. If desired, type more search words or phrases and a search location.

6. If you've entered more than one search string, choose a boolean operator in the submenu. Choose And to find pages that contain *both* search words or phrases. Choose Or to find pages with *either* one word or phrase *or the other*.

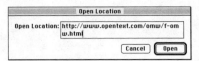

Figure 6.8 *Type Open Text's URL in the Open Location dialog box.*

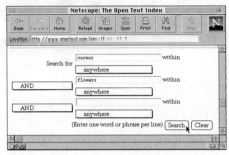

Figure 6.9 *Type the criteria (first* cosmos *and then* flowers. *If desired, choose a boolean operator like AND or OR and a place. Then click Search. In this example, we used AND to make sure that the pages found would be about Cosmos flowers and not about the starry cosmos.*

Figure 6.10 *Open Text lists the results, giving the name of the page, its size, its score (how well it satisfied the search criteria, and the page's address.*

Searching for Web pages by keyword

Figure 6.11 *Each found page gives several options: Visit the page, See matches on the page, and Find similar pages. You can also click the page's title to jump to it.*

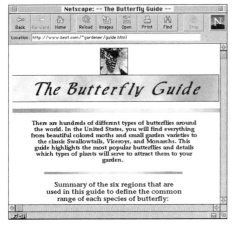

Figure 6.12 *The desired page is shown in the browser.*

7. Click Search to start the search. (Click Clear to start over from scratch.) Open Text shows the links to the pages that satisfied the search criteria **(Figure 6.10)**.

8. Under each found page, you'll have three choices **(Figure 6.11)**. Click View page (or the title itself) to jump to that page **(Figure 6.12)**. Choose See Matches on this page to see where the search word(s) appear on the page without jumping to it. Choose Find similar pages to have Open Text analyze how the search criteria appear on the page and then find pages with a similar relationship.

✔ Tips

- Make sure you spell the keyword(s) correctly. If you type "Catchmear" when looking for lush, goat fiber, you are likely to be disappointed.

- Add word endings to make a search more complete. If you type "fiber" don't expect to find "fibers".

- Use a space to make searches more specific. Open Text finds all the pages that *begin* with the typed word. So if you type "straw" you'll also find "strawberry". But if you type "straw " with a space after the *w*, you'll only find "straw".

- Lycos *(http://www.lycos.com)*, Excite *(http://www.excite.com)*, and Altavista *(http://altavista.digital.com)* are three other word-based Web search services.

- To use Netscape's search services, choose Internet Directory, Internet Search and Internet White Pages in the Directory menu (or with the Directory buttons).

Searching for Web pages by keyword

Searching for people and organizations

Remember Marcy from college? Haven't talked to her lately? Maybe you can find her. Although there's no centralized white pages (at least not for free), there are services that attempt to track down and index e-mail addresses.

To search for a person's e-mail address:

1. Choose Open Location or click the Open button on the toolbar.

2. Type **whowhere** in the text box and click Open to display the WhoWhere? home page **(Fig. 6.13)**. You can search by person or by organization.

3. If you're looking for a person, type the person's name in the text box in the middle frame.

4. If desired, scroll down to enter information about the person's organization, or location.

5. Click the Search button—you may have to scroll down in the middle frame to find it. WhoWhere? displays the results as links, and divides them into three categories: highly, probably and possibly relevant **(Figure 6.14)**.

✔ Tips

- Click on a person's address to send her an e-mail message right away.

- To save an address, press the mouse button and select Copy this Link Location in the submenu. Save the address as described on page 126.

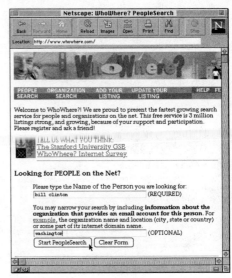

Figure 6.13 *Type the person's name (and their organization or location, if you know it) and then click Start People Search.*

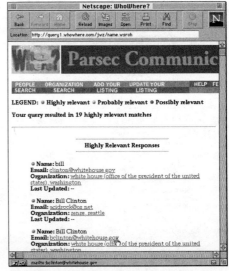

Figure 6.14 *Scroll through the list of matches to see if the person you were looking for is there. Click their name to send them an e-mail message.*

Figure 6.15 *To start a search for an organization, click Organization search at the top of the page.*

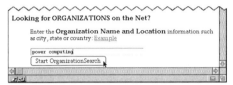

Figure 6.16 *Enter the name of the organization.*

Figure 6.17 *Click the desired organization to see its home page.*

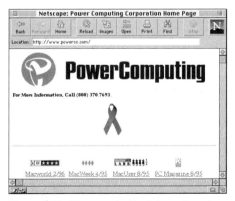

Figure 6.18 *The organization's home page is displayed in the browser.*

You can also use WhoWhere? to look for an organizations' Web site. Although many organizations have guessable URLs in the form of *www.organization.com*, others do not. WhoWhere? bridges the gap.

To find an organization:

1. Follow steps 1 and 2 on the previous page.

2. Click Organization Search in the top frame of the WhoWhere? home page **(Figure 6.15)**.

3. Type the name of the organization, and if desired, its location (city or state) in the text box **(Figure 6.16)**.

4. Click the Search button or press Return. WhoWhere? shows you the links to the pages that satisfy the search criteria **(Figure 6.17)**.

5. Click on the desired link. (Links to organizations tend to be Web pages as opposed to e-mail addresses.) The newly found page is displayed **(Figure 6.18)**.

✔ Tip

■ Before doing a search, try typing **www.organization.com** in the Open Location dialog box or in the Location field, where *organization* is the name of the company you're looking for.

Finding an article in a newsgroup

There are over 14,000 newsgroups, and each of them receives from several to several hundred messages a day. Finding a message that deals with a particular topic can be difficult. You can use Deja News to search for newsgroup messages.

To do a quick search for an article in a newsgroup:

1. Choose Open Location or click the Open button on the toolbar.

2. Type **dejanews** in the text box and click Open.

3. In the Deja News home page that appears, type the search criteria, and click the Find button **(Figure 6.19)**.

4. Deja News lists the articles that fit the criteria **(Figure 6.20)**. Click an article that interests you to view that message. The message is shown in the browser, not the News window **(Figure 6.21)**.

5. If desired, you can reply to the posting by clicking Post Article. You'll be automatically switched to the News window. Or, e-mail a response to the writer by clicking Email Reply. A regular Message Composition window will appear.

✔ Tip

■ You can also refine requests further by clicking Power Search at the top of Deja News' home page.

Figure 6.19 *In Deja News' home page, type the search criteria and click Find.*

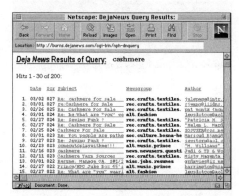

Figure 6.20 *By default, the articles are listed in abbreviated form. Click the desired article to read it.*

Figure 6.21 *Click the desired listing and Deja News shows you the entire message. Click on Post Article to jump to the newsgroup. Click Email Reply to send a message to the sender.*

Finding an article in a newsgroup

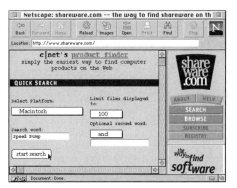

Figure 6.22 *In the main Search window, choose the appropriate platform, the keywords (in this example, Speed Bump), the number of files you wish to display and an optional second keyword. Then click Start Search.*

Figure 6.23 *The shareware programs or updates that satisfy the criteria given in the Search window (Figure 6.22) are listed in the central frame. Click one to see the available FTP sites.*

Figure 6.24 *When you click a file to download, shareware.com lists the FTP sites where you can find it. Click an FTP site to download the file.*

Finding shareware through the Web

Sometimes, the hardest part about downloading a file is finding it. One service that provides you with the FTP addresses for over 160,000 shareware programs (as well as commercial software updates) is shareware.com by C/net.

To find shareware through the Web:

1. Choose Open Location or click the Open button on the toolbar.

2. Type **shareware** in the text box and click Open. The C/net home page appears.

3. Click Search in either the left or top right frame to begin.

4. Choose the desired platform in the Select platform submenu **(Fig. 6.22)**.

5. Type the appropriate keywords in the Search word submenu.

6. If desired, type a second key word and select And or Or.

7. Click Start search. The shareware files that satisfy the criteria given are listed in the central frame **(Figure 6.23)**.

8. Click the desired file to list the FTP sites where it can be found as well as its approximate download time **(Figure 6.24)**.

9. Click the desired FTP site to download the file. For more information on FTP transfers, consult *Downloading files* on page 42.

Finding information in an open page

You've been reading this whole chapter thinking to yourself, "Hah, I know an easier way. What about the Find button on the toolbar?" The problem with the Find button is that it only searches within a particular page (or the image in print). It doesn't search out on the Web. So, if you're looking for a particular word or phrase within a long document that you're already viewing, that's when you should use the Find button.

To find information in an open page:

1. Jump to the desired page **(Fig. 6.25)**.

2. Click the Find button on the toolbar or choose Find in the Edit menu **(Figure 6.26)**. The Find dialog box appears.

3. Type the word or phrase that you wish to look for and click Find **(Figure 6.27)**. Netscape will highlight the first occurrence of the word, if any, in the currently open page **(Figure 6.28)**.

4. If desired, choose Find Again in the Edit menu to find the next occurrence of the search word or phrase **(Figure 6.29)**.

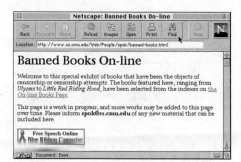

Figure 6.25 *Once you've found the page that you think contains the information, click the Find button to jump to the desired text.*

Figure 6.26 *You can also choose Find in the Edit menu.*

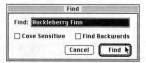

Figure 6.27 *Type the text you're looking for and click Find.*

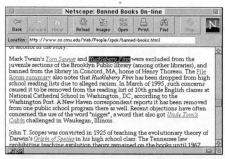

Figure 6.28 *Netscape highlights the found text. If this is the text you want, you're all set. Otherwise, choose Find Again in the Edit menu to find the next occurrence of the text.*

Figure 6.29 *Choose Find Again in the Edit menu to find the next occurrence of the text in the open page.*

Finding information in an open page

Figure 6.30 *Choose Netscape's Home in the Directory menu to jump to Netscape Corporation's home page.*

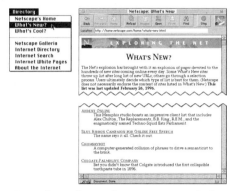

Figure 6.31 *Choose What's New? to see which sites Netscape has discovered lately.*

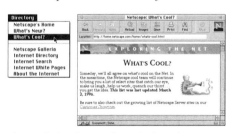

Figure 6.32 *Choose What's Cool? in the Directory menu to see what Netscape Corporation considers a "cool" page.*

Figure 6.33 *You can also choose What's New? and What's Cool? (among other things) with the Directory buttons. Personally, I think they take up too much window space. To hide them, consult Controlling a browser's appearance on page 15.*

Checking out Netscape's pages

Some of Netscape's menu commands take you to particular pages on the Web (mostly on Netscape's own site). Some of these sites are kind of helpful. Some are less so.

To find Netscape's home page:

Choose Netscape's Home in the Directory menu **(Figure 6.30)** or click the Netscape icon at the right side of the browser.

To find new pages (according to Netscape):

Choose What's New? in the Directory menu or click the What's New? button at the top of the browser **(Figure 6.31 and Figure 6.33)**.

To find cool pages (according to Netscape):

Choose What's Cool? in the Directory menu or click the What's Cool? button at the top of the browser **(Figure 6.32 and Figure 6.33)**.

To find servers built with Netscape servers software:

Choose Netscape Galleria in the Directory menu.

To search the Web with Netscape's search service:

Choose Internet Directory, Internet Search or Internet White Pages in the Directory menu. (For more information on finding Web pages, read the rest of this chapter.)

Finding Netscape documentation

A couple of Netscape's built-in commands link you to help pages, including the documentation for Netscape itself.

To find the Netscape handbook:

Choose Handbook in the Help menu **(Figure 6.34)** or click the Handbook button at the top of the browser. Netscape's documentation will be displayed. This is the same documentation you would get if you bought the manuals—although perhaps more up-to-date.

FAQ, which rhymes with *smack* and stands for Frequently Asked Questions, is a list of questions that Netscape has received over and over again. Your question may or may not be among them. Answers are included.

To find the Netscape FAQ:

1. Choose Frequently Asked Questions in the Help menu **(Figure 6.35)**.

2. Click the Netscape Navigator FAQ link. Netscape's FAQs on Navigator are divided into several files.

3. Click on the FAQ link that interests you.

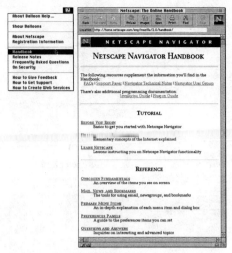

Figure 6.34 *Choose Handbook in the Help menu (at the far right of your screen) to view the latest version of Netscape's documentation.*

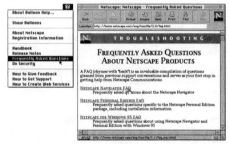

Figure 6.35 *Choose Frequently Asked Questions in the Help menu (at the far right of your screen) to see a file with the questions (and answers) that Netscape receives most often.*

Figure 6.36 *Choose Open Location in the File menu (or click the Open button in the toolbar).*

Figure 6.37 *Type the URL address for the support request form in the Open Location dialog box.*

Figure 6.38 *Fill out the Client Help Request Form (it's long) and then click the Submit this problem button at the bottom of the page.*

Finding technical support

Netscape offers free technical support by telephone to users who have bought the Personal Edition of Netscape Navigator, or for users who have downloaded the LAN version by modem and then registered and paid for it. If you have not paid for Netscape, they will charge you $25 for the first 15 minutes, plus $2 for each additional minute.

To find technical support by telephone:

Call 1-800-320-2099.

Only registered LAN version Netscape users can get support via e-mail.

To find technical support online:

1. Choose Open Location in the File menu **(Figure 6.36)** or click the Open button. The Open Location dialog box appears **(Figure 6.37)**.

2. Type **http://home.netscape.com/ assist/support/client/help.html**.

3. Fill out the form **(Figure 6.38)**.

4. Click Submit this problem at the bottom of the page. As long as you are a registered LAN version Netscape user, you should receive a notification in a couple of hours and a response within a few days.

✔ Tip

■ If you choose How to Get Support from the Help menu, you'll get referred to the handbook and the FAQs before you finally reach the form shown in Figure 6.38.

Finding technical support

Finding info about your Netscape software

Netscape's menus offer ways to get information about the software itself. You can find out what version you have, what plug-ins you have installed, what your registration number is, what upgrade options you have, and what new features have been added to the program since your version was released.

To get information about your Netscape software:

1. Choose About Netscape in the Help menu (or in the Apple menu). The version number of your software is displayed **(Figure 6.39)**.

2. Click in the Netscape logo (in the About Netscape page) to see information about the software engineers who developed Netscape.

3. Choose Registration Information in the Help menu. Your registration number is displayed **(Figure 6.40)**. If you have not yet registered your copy of Netscape, information on how to register will be shown.

4. Choose Release Notes in the Help menu. A list of the new features included in your copy of Netscape appears **(Figure 6.41)**.

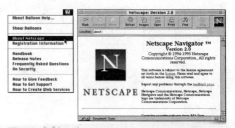

Figure 6.39 *Choose About Netscape in the Help menu (at the far right of your screen) to see what version of the program you are using.*

Figure 6.40 *Choose Registration to see your registration ID or to register the program.*

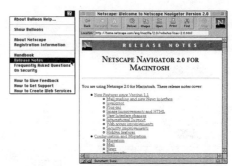

Figure 6.41 *Choose Release Notes to see a list of new features for your version of Netscape.*

Finding info about your Netscape software

Bookmarks

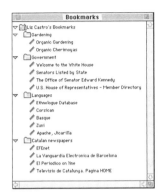

Figure 7.1 *The Bookmarks window helps you organize your favorite sites and get back to them with a simple double click.*

Figure 7.2 *In the Bookmarks menu, choose the page you wish to jump to.*

Figure 7.3 *To open the Bookmarks window, choose Bookmarks in the Window menu.*

What is a bookmark?

There are approximately 4 million Web pages already in existence. If someday you should find a link to a gem of a page, you won't want to lose it. With Netscape you can store the URL addresses to your favorite sites as *bookmarks*. The next time you want to jump to that site, instead of trying to remember the circuitous route you took the first time, simply pull up your Bookmarks window, double click and sail in. Or surf. Whatever.

The bookmarks that you create are listed in the Bookmarks window, which you can display on screen or hide at your convenience **(Figure 7.1)**. They are also listed at the bottom of the Bookmarks menu for easy access **(Figure 7.2)**.

To open the Bookmarks window:

Choose Bookmarks in the Window menu **(Figure 7.3)**.

Using bookmarks to navigate the Web

Bookmarks make it easy to find your way back to favorite sites. The truth is, typing URLs is a pain. It's easy to mix up lower and upper case letters, leave off a back slash, or simply misspell part of the address. Navigating with bookmarks is a breeze—double click and you're there.

To navigate with the Bookmarks window:

1. Choose Bookmarks in the Window menu. The Bookmarks window appears.

2. Double click the bookmark to jump to the corresponding Web page. You may also click once on the bookmark and choose Go to Bookmark in the Item menu (**Figure 7.4 and Figure 7.5**). The page is displayed in the browser (**Figure 7.7**).

To navigate with the Bookmarks menu:

1. Choose the desired Web page from the Bookmarks menu (**Figure 7.6**). The page is displayed in the browser (**Figure 7.7**).

✔ Tip

■ Double click a folder in the Bookmarks window to open it and see its contents or to close it and hide its contents. You can tell that a folder is open by the arrow to its right. If the arrow points to the folder, the folder is closed. If the arrow points down, the folder is open.

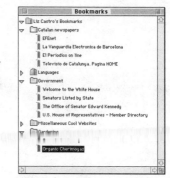

Figure 7.4 *Select a bookmark in the Bookmarks window.*

Figure 7.5 *Choose Go to Bookmark in the Item menu.*

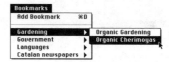

Figure 7.6 *The Bookmarks menu lets you navigate to your favorite sites without pulling up the Bookmarks window.*

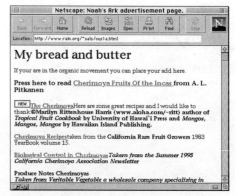

Figure 7.7 *The chosen page is displayed in the browser.*

70

Figure 7.8 *With the Bookmarks window active, choose What's New? in the File menu.*

Figure 7.9 *Choose All bookmarks or Selected bookmarks and then click Start Checking.*

Figure 7.10 *While Netscape connects to each of the sites in your bookmarks file, it gives you a progress report. Click Stop Checking to cancel the search.*

Figure 7.11 *Once Netscape has finished checking each of the sites in your bookmarks file, it gives you a final report.*

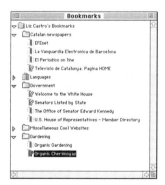

Figure 7.12 *The sites with new material are marked with "bright" marks. Sites that Netscape was unable to contact are indicated with a question mark.*

Checking what's new

Netscape can look through all your bookmarks, or through a selected group of them, and tell which pages have changed since your last visit.

To check what's new:

1. If desired, choose the bookmarks that you wish to check.

2. Choose What's New? in the Bookmarks window's File menu **(Figure 7.8)**. The What's New? dialog box appears.

3. If you made a selection of bookmarks, click Selected Bookmarks. Otherwise, leave All Bookmarks checked **(Figure 7.9)**. Click OK. Netscape connects to each of the pages listed in your bookmarks file to see if they've changed since your last visit.

4. A dialog box appears that charts Netscape's progress **(Figure 7.10)**. Click Stop Checking if you get tired of waiting. Netscape gives you a final report **(Figure 7.11)**. Click Stop Checking to close the dialog box. Then Netscape displays changed bookmarks with "bright" marks **(Figure 7.12)**. Bookmarks that Netscape was unable to analyze are indicated with a question mark.

✔ **Tip**

■ When you create a bookmark manually, Netscape marks it with a question mark, indicating that you have not visited it.

Setting the New Bookmarks folder

When you add a bookmark, it is automatically appended to the New Bookmarks folder in the current bookmarks file. By default, Netscape sets up the principal folder to receive new bookmarks. However, you can choose any folder as the receiving folder, making it easy to add several bookmarks at a time to a particular category.

To set the New Bookmarks folder:

1. Click once on the folder to which new bookmarks should be added when you use the Add Bookmark command in the Bookmarks menu. You may choose any folder at any level in the Bookmarks window.

2. Choose Set to New Bookmarks Folder in the Item menu **(Figure 7.13)**. The new New Bookmarks folder is indicated by a folder with the bookmark icon inside it **(Figure 7.14)**.

Figure 7.13 *Choose the folder that you want to add new bookmarks to and then choose Set to New Bookmarks Folder in the Item menu.*

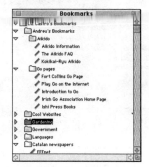

Figure 7.14 *A blue bookmark icon appears on top of the folder that you have designated as the New Bookmarks folder.*

Figure 7.15 *To select a new folder from which the Bookmarks menu will be generated, click the desired folder to select it and then choose Set to Bookmark Menu Folder in the Item menu.*

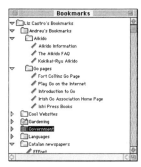

Figure 7.16 *The new Bookmarks menu folder has a menu icon on top of the folder icon.*

Figure 7.17 *The Bookmarks menu shows only those bookmarks that are contained in the folder that you've designated as the Bookmarks menu folder.*

Setting the Bookmarks menu folder

The Bookmarks menu is generated from the bookmarks in the Bookmarks window in order to give you rapid access to your bookmarks. You can choose which folder in the Bookmarks window is used to create the menu.

To set the Bookmarks menu folder:

1. Click once on the folder from which you want to generate the Bookmarks menu. You can choose any folder at any level of the Bookmarks window.

2. Choose Set to Bookmark Menu Folder in the Item menu **(Figure 7.15)**. A menu icon appears on top of the folder icon **(Figure 7.16)**.

3. Display the Bookmarks menu to see the new configuration **(Figure 7.17)**.

✔ Tip

- OK, this isn't really a tip, just a complaint. The menu is called "Bookmarks" not "Bookmark" so why is the option called "Set to Bookmark Menu Folder"? Ask Netscape.

Setting the Bookmarks menu folder

Adding a bookmark from a Web site

The hardest part about creating a bookmark is finding a page that is worth going back to. Once you are there, adding a reference to the page is a snap.

To add a bookmark:

1. Navigate to the page whose URL you wish to save.

2. Choose Add Bookmark in the Bookmarks menu **(Figure 7.18)**. The title and URL of the Web page that you are currently browsing will be saved in a bookmark in the New Bookmarks folder *(see page 72)* and will be automatically appended to the Bookmarks menu **(Figure 7.19)**.

✔ Tips

- You can also drag links from a page (or mail message or news posting) to the Bookmarks window.

- Click a link and then choose Add Bookmark for this Link in the pop-up menu to add a link from a page without going to the page.

- When you add a link by dragging or choosing Add Bookmark for this Link in the pop-up menu, the URL (and not the title of the page) is used as the bookmark title. For information on changing the bookmark's title, consult *Editing a bookmark or folder* on page 78.

- When you create a bookmark, make sure it goes directly to the page you want, and not just to the site's home page.

Figure 7.18 *Once you have found a good page, simply choose Add Bookmark (Command-D) in the Bookmarks menu to add the page to your bookmarks file.*

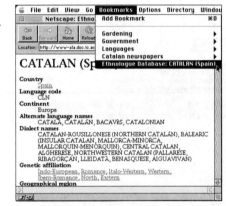

Figure 7.19 *The current page's title and URL are immediately added to the Bookmarks menu (as shown) and to the Bookmarks window.*

Figure 7.20 *Choose Insert Bookmark in the Item menu to open the New Bookmark dialog box.*

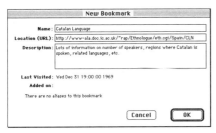

Figure 7.21 *The New Bookmark dialog box (identical to the Bookmark Properties dialog box) contains information about the Title, URL and Description of a bookmark, as well as the last date you visited the site.*

Adding a bookmark by hand

You don't need to connect to a page in order to add it to your bookmark file. As long as you know a page's URL—perhaps you've found a reference in a magazine— you can create a bookmark for the page manually.

Adding a bookmark by hand:

1. Open the Bookmarks window by choosing Bookmarks in the Window menu. The Bookmarks window appears.

2. Choose Insert Bookmark in the Item menu **(Figure 7.20)**. The New Bookmark dialog box appears **(Fig. 7.21)**.

3. Type a title for the new bookmark in the Name text box. This title will appear in the Go menu and in the Bookmarks window.

4. Type (or copy) the URL for the page in the Location (URL) text box.

5. Finally, if desired, enter a short description of the page in the Description text box.

6. Click OK to add the bookmark to your bookmarks file.

✔ Tips

■ Type upper and lower case letters in URLs exactly as they were, and beware of typos.

■ You can add bookmarks manually without connecting to the Internet thereby saving connect time and phone charges.

■ Hold down the Option key while you double click a bookmark to open the Bookmark Properties dialog box.

Adding a bookmark by hand

Creating aliases of bookmarks

An alias is a sort of remote control. You can create aliases of your bookmarks in order to have access to your favorite sites in several locations in your bookmarks file. You use an alias exactly the same way you use a regular bookmark. The big difference is that if you change the URL or description of the original bookmark, the corresponding aliases are updated automatically.

Figure 7.22 *After selecting the source book-mark, choose Make Alias in the Item menu.*

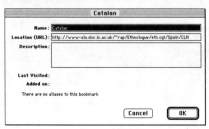

Figure 7.23 *The only field you can modify in the Bookmark Properties dialog box of an alias is the Title. The URL and description are generated from the source bookmark.*

To create an alias:

1. Click once on the bookmark that you wish to create an alias of.

2. Choose Make Alias in the Item menu **(Figure 7.22)**. The alias appears below the original bookmark. Aliases are shown in italics in the Bookmarks window to distinguish them from regular bookmarks.

3. Drag the alias to the new location.

4. If desired, edit the alias to give it a new name or description **(Fig. 7.23)**. For more information, consult *Editing a bookmark or folder* on page 78.

✔ Tips

■ You may not edit an alias' URL, since it comes directly from the bookmark. To change an alias' URL, change the URL of the *source* bookmark.

■ If you change a bookmark's description, you won't see the change in the alias' Bookmark Properties dialog box. However, if you open the bookmarks file as a Web page *(see page 83)*, the description will be updated correctly.

Figure 7.24 *To create a new folder for organizing your bookmarks, choose Insert Folder in the Item menu.*

Figure 7.25 *Use the New Header dialog box to change the Title and Description of folders as well as bookmarks. You cannot associate a URL with a folder. (It wouldn't make sense anyway.)*

Figure 7.26 *The new folder appears directly below the folder you selected before choosing the Insert Folder command.*

Creating a bookmark folder

If you have a lot of bookmarks, sooner or later you will find that searching through your list is almost as troublesome as searching through the Web. The solution is a little organization. You can categorize your bookmarks and separate them into named folders.

To create a bookmark folder:

1. Open the Bookmarks window by choosing Bookmarks in the Window menu. The Bookmarks window appears. If you haven't created any folders yet, all the bookmarks will be in the default folder that Netscape creates for you.

2. Select the folder in which you wish to create the new folder.

3. Choose Insert Folder in the Item menu **(Figure 7.24)**. The New Header dialog box appears **(Figure 7.25)**.

4. In the Name field, type the name for your new folder.

5. In the Description field, enter a few words that define your category. This is a good way to help you remember what goes in this folder which, in turn, makes the folder more useful.

6. Click OK. The new folder appears in the Bookmarks window, below—that is, *inside*—the principal folder **(Figure 7.26)**.

7. Drag bookmarks or other folders to the new folder.

Creating a bookmark folder

Editing a bookmark or folder

When you add a bookmark with the Add Bookmark command, the title of the page is automatically used in the Bookmarks window to identify the bookmark. You may wish to give the bookmark a name that more clearly identifies its contents. In addition, you can change a bookmark's URL (perhaps, the creators of the page have moved it to a new server) or change its description.

Figure 7.27 *Choose Edit Bookmark in the Item menu to display the Bookmark Properties dialog box.*

Figure 7.28 *In the Bookmark Properties window, you may change the Title to better identify the page's contents; update a page's URL or add a description for the page.*

To edit a bookmark:

1. Open the Bookmarks window by choosing Bookmarks in the Window menu. The Bookmarks window appears.

2. Click once on the bookmark that you wish to edit. Choose Edit Bookmark in the Item menu **(Fig. 7.27)**. You can also hold down the Option key as you double click the bookmark. The Bookmark Properties dialog box appears **(Figure 7.28)**.

3. Change the Name, URL, and Description in the corresponding text boxes as desired.

4. Click OK to save the changes. The bookmark's information is automatically updated in the Bookmarks window **(Figure 7.29)**.

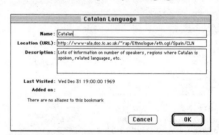

Figure 7.29 *Once you click OK to save the changes, the new data is automatically updated in both the Bookmarks window and the Bookmarks menu.*

✔ Tip

- To delete a bookmark or folder (or separator) that you don't use anymore, select it and choose Delete Bookmark in the Edit menu **(Figure 7.30)** or press Command-Delete.

Figure 7.30 *To delete a bookmark, select it in the Bookmarks window and then choose Delete Bookmark in the Edit menu. You can also select the bookmark and then press Command-Delete (not the Del key).*

Figure 7.31 *To add a separator, first select the bookmark or folder below which you wish to insert the separator.*

Figure 7.32 *Choose Insert Separator in the Item menu.*

Figure 7.33 *In the Bookmarks window, the separator appears as a dashed line.*

Figure 7.34 *The separator appears below the currently selected item. You may insert separators at any level of the bookmarks hierarchy.*

Adding a separator

If you have several folders, it may be help-ful to have a visual clue that separates them. Since the Bookmarks menu is gen-erated from your Bookmarks window, the separators that you include in the window will also appear in the menu.

To add a separator to your bookmarks window:

1. Click once on the folder or bookmark directly above the place where you wish to insert a separator **(Fig. 7.31)**.

2. Choose Insert Separator in the Item menu **(Figure 7.32)**. A dashed line appears in the desired location **(Figure 7.33)**.

3. Click on the Bookmarks menu to see your new separator **(Figure 7.34)**.

✔ Tip

■ You are not limited to adding separa-tors only between folders. You can insert a separator between any two objects in the Bookmarks window, regardless of their levels.

Adding a separator

Sorting your bookmarks file

If you have more than five or six bookmarks in a folder, or more than five or six
folders in your bookmarks file, you may
wish to alphabetize the items to make
them easier to find.

To sort your bookmarks:

1. Click once in the folder whose bookmarks or subfolders you wish to sort
   (**Figure 7.35**).

2. Choose Sort Bookmarks in the Item
   menu (**Figure 7.36**). All of the folders and bookmarks in the selected
   folder will be sorted alphabetically
   (**Figure 7.37**). Separators are placed
   at the top of the list. Items within folders other than the selected folder are
   not sorted.

✔ Tips

- If you want to sort all of your bookmarks and folders, click in the principal folder at the top of your
  Bookmarks window.

- You can undo a sort; simply choose
  Undo in the Edit menu.

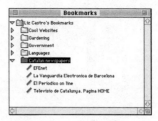

Figure 7.35 *Click once on a folder to select it for sorting.*

Figure 7.36 *Choose Sort Bookmarks in the Item menu.*

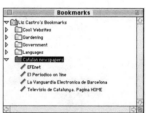

Figure 7.37 *The bookmarks are sorted alphabetically, in descending order, without losing the organization in folders.*

Figure 7.38 *To save a bookmarks file, perhaps to share it with friends or as a backup, choose Save Bookmark File As in the File menu.*

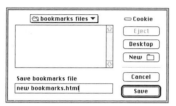

Figure 7.39 *In the standard Save dialog box that appears, type the name for the new bookmarks file.*

Saving a bookmarks file

You can save a bookmarks file to give to friends, or simply to make a back-up copy. In fact, a bookmarks file is nothing more than an HTML page that you can browse as you would any other local file.

To save a bookmark file:

1. Choose Save Bookmark File As in the File menu **(Figure 7.38)**. A standard Save As dialog box appears.

2. Give the file a name and choose the folder in which to save it **(Fig. 7.39)**.

3. Click OK to save the file.

✔ Tips

■ If you tack on the extension .html to the end of your bookmark file's name, you'll be able to open the file as a regular Web page *(see page 83)* and share it with other Mac and Unix users. If you give it the .htm extension, you'll be able to read the file with a browser on a PC.

■ For example, if you save your bookmarks file with the proper extension (.html), you'll be able to designate it as your home page. This way, each time you open Netscape, you will have your favorite sites just a click away. For more information, consult *Choosing a home page* on page 14.

Saving a bookmarks file

Opening a different bookmarks file

Although your bookmarks file is hidden from view when you close the Bookmarks window, it is not gone. Simply open the window again to see the bookmarks file again. If, however, you wish to open a *different bookmarks file*, you must follow these steps.

Figure 7.40 *The default bookmarks file (Bookmarks.html) can be found in the Netscape f folder, inside the Preferences folder inside the System Folder.*

To open a different bookmarks file:

1. Choose Quit in the File menu to close Netscape.

2. Find the Netscape folder in the Preferences folder inside the System folder on your start-up disk **(Figure 7.40)**.

3. Drag the bookmarks.html file out of the Netscape folder.

4. Change the name of the new bookmarks file to bookmarks.html and place it in the Netscape folder.

5. Double click Netscape to open it.

6. Choose Bookmarks in the Window menu. The new bookmarks file will be displayed.

✔ Tip

■ Saving and opening multiple bookmarks files is an ideal way to share hot site addresses. Since the bookmarks file is nothing more than a simple HTML file, you can also open it directly with Netscape—on PCs, Macs or even Unix machines—no matter what kind of computer the bookmark file comes from. *(See "Opening a bookmarks file as a Web page" on page 83.)*

Figure 7.41 *To open a bookmarks file as a Web page, choose Open File in the File menu.*

Figure 7.42 *Find the bookmarks file you wish to open as a Web page, and double click it (or click it once and click Open).*

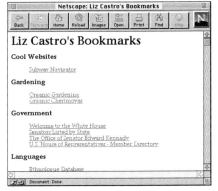

Figure 7.43 *The bookmarks file, complete with links to your saved sites, appears just like any other Web page.*

Opening a bookmarks file as a Web page

An easy way to see a bookmarks file without changing your regular bookmarks file is to open it as a Web page. Since the bookmarks file is in HTML format, like any other Web page, Netscape knows how to interpret it correctly, displaying folders in a large font, and making your bookmarks into links—automatically.

To open a bookmarks file as a Web page:

1. Save your bookmarks file. For more information, consult *Saving a bookmarks file* on page 81.

2. Choose Open File in the File menu **(Figure 7.41)**.

3. Choose the desired file and click Open **(Figure 7.42)**. The bookmarks file is loaded into Netscape just like any other Web page **(Figure 7.43)**.

✔ Tip

■ You can also designate a bookmarks file as a home page so that Netscape displays it automatically every time you launch the program, giving you immediate access to frequently visited sites. For more information, consult *Choosing a home page* on page 14.

Opening a bookmarks file as a Web page

Importing bookmarks

If you wish, you may *add* the bookmarks in a bookmarks file to your current bookmarks file, instead of replacing the existing bookmarks.

To import bookmarks:

1. Open the Bookmarks windows by choosing Bookmarks in the Window menu. The Bookmarks window appears.

2. Choose Import Bookmarks in the File menu **(Figure 7.44)**. The Import dialog box appears.

3. Choose the bookmarks file that you wish to import and click Open **(Fig. 7.45)**. The bookmarks in the imported file are added to the current Bookmarks window **(Figure 7.46)**.

Figure 7.44 *To add a bookmarks file's bookmarks to the current bookmarks file, choose Import Bookmarks in the File menu.*

Figure 7.45 *In the Import dialog box that appears, select the bookmarks file you wish to import and click Open.*

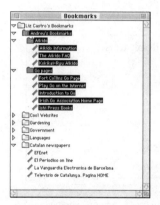

Figure 7.46 *The new bookmarks are added below the main folder in the current bookmarks file. The existing bookmarks are not affected.*

Importing bookmarks

Part II:
Mail and News

The Mail Window

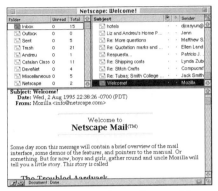

Figure 8.1 *You can change the size of the three panes in the Mail window, making them taller or shorter, or wider or narrower, according to the particular task at hand.*

The Mail window is Netscape's central filing area for all incoming and outgoing correspondence. From the Mail window, you can get, read and send new mail, respond to mail, delete mail, and file mail.

Not all mail is equal. The Mail window lets you flag important letters and marks all mail as read or unread, letting you choose to list all mail, or only that correspondence which you have not yet read.

The Mail window's filing system is fairly advanced, allowing you to create new folders for organizing incoming and outgoing correspondence, and to throw away those letters you no longer need.

Before you use the Mail or News windows, fill out the Server *(see page 168)* and Identity information *(see page 169)*.

The parts of the Mail window

The Mail window is divided into three areas, or panes **(Figure 8.1)**. The top left pane contains the folders in which your mail is organized. New mail is automatically filed in the Inbox folder. Outgoing mail that has not yet been sent is filed in the Outbox folder.

When you click in one of the mail folders, a list of the messages contained in the folder appears in the top right pane of the Mail window. Each letter is identified by its Subject, Sender, Date, and whether it has been marked or read.

Once you click in one of the e-mail messages, the contents of the letter appear in the bottom pane.

Opening the Mail window

The Mail window, together with the Browser and News windows, forms one leg of the Netscape triumvirate. You can have each type of window open at once, but to work with mail, the Mail window must be open and active.

To open the Mail window:

1. Choose Netscape Mail in the Window menu **(Figure 8.2)**. Netscape automatically checks your mail.

2. If the password dialog box appears, enter your password and click OK **(Figure 8.3)**. The Mail window appears **(Figure 8.4)**.

✔ Tip

■ You can also click the letter icon in the bottom right corner of all Netscape's windows to open the Mail window.

Saving your mail password

You can save your mail password so that Netscape doesn't ask for it each time you open the Mail window.

To save your Mail password:

1. Choose Mail and News Preferences in the Options menu **(Figure 8.5)**.

2. Click the Organization tab. The Organization preferences appear.

3. Click Remember Mail Password at the top of the dialog box **(Figure 8.6)**.

4. Click OK.

Figure 8.2 *To open the Mail window, choose Netscape Mail in the Window menu.*

Figure 8.3 *If the Password Entry dialog box appears, enter your password and click OK.*

Figure 8.4 *The Mail window has three panes. The top left pane shows the folders, the top right pane shows the letters in each folder and the bottom pane shows the contents of each letter.*

Figure 8.5 *Choose Mail and News Preferences in the Options menu.*

Figure 8.6 *Click the Organization tab and then click Remember Mail Password.*

Opening the Mail window

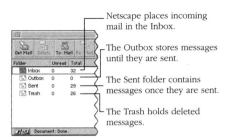

Netscape places incoming mail in the Inbox.

The Outbox stores messages until they are sent.

The Sent folder contains messages once they are sent.

The Trash holds deleted messages.

Figure 8.7 *The Mail window contains four folders by default. You may add others as desired.*

The Mail window's four default folders

Netscape creates four default folders for filing mail: the Inbox, the Outbox, the Sent, and the Trash folders **(Figure 8.7)**.

Netscape stores the new, incoming mail in the Inbox. Once you've read them, you can move them to a more specific folder *(see page 95)*. Or if you're lazy like me, you can just leave them there.

The Outbox holds mail that you've written but haven't yet sent. For example, you can write several messages without being connected to your Internet server and then send them all at once *(see page 112)*. If you change your mind about sending a message, simply move it from the Outbox folder.

Once you've actually sent a message, Netscape transfers it to the Sent folder. You can choose to file sent messages in another folder, or just leave them there.

Finally, the Trash folder holds mail that you've deleted. For more information on deleting files, consult *Deleting messages and folders* on page 96. You can retrieve messages from the Trash (it doesn't even smell bad) until you decide to empty it. Once you've emptied the trash *(see page 97)*, the messages are truly gone.

The Mail window's four default folders

Creating new folders

In addition to Netscape's default folders *(see page 89)*, you can create as many of your own as your hard disk space will allow. Folders are helpful for organizing your mail once you've received or sent it.

To create a new folder:

1. In the File menu, choose New Folder **(Figure 8.8)**.

2. Enter a name for the folder in the dialog box that appears and click OK **(Figure 8.9)**. The new folder appears in the left pane of the Mail window **(Figure 8.10)**.

✔ Tips

■ You can't create a folder inside another folder.

■ It's a little tricky to change a folder's name once it's created. The easiest way is to create a new folder with the correct name and drag any messages to the new folder. The hard way is by finding the desired mail folder file (usually in the Mail folder inside the Netscape folder inside the Preferences folder in your System folder on your hard disk) and changing the name of both it and the corresponding .snm file.

■ The Add Folder command is not for adding new folders, but rather for importing the contents of one folder into another. For more information, consult *Importing messages from another folder* on page 92.

■ If the New Folder command doesn't appear, make sure the Mail window is active.

Figure 8.8 *Choose New Folder in the File menu.*

Figure 8.9 *In the dialog box that appears, type a name for the new folder and click OK.*

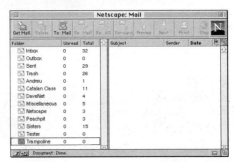

Figure 8.10 *The new folder appears in the left pane of the Mail window.*

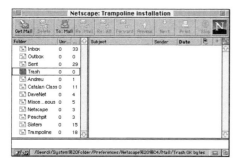

Figure 8.11 *Before nesting folders, each folder is at the same level.*

Figure 8.12 *Open the Mail folder (inside the Netscape folder, inside the Preferences folder, inside the System folder on your start-up disk).*

Figure 8.13 *Create new folders in the Mail folder and drag the existing folders (in the form of files) to the desired locations.*

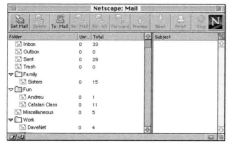

Figure 8.14 *The folders in the Mail window reflect the hierarchy of the folders in the Mail folder on your hard disk.*

Nesting folders

There is no menu command for creating folders inside an existing folder. However, if you know how to create folders on your Mac, you can create nested folders in the Mail window.

To create nested folders:

1. Close the Mail window.

2. Switch to the Finder.

3. Open the Mail folder, which is inside the Netscape folder, inside the Preferences folder, inside the System folder **(Figure 8.12)**.

4. Choose New Folder in the Finder's File menu to create new folders as desired inside the Mail folder.

5. Organize the existing folders (which appear as files—one with and one without the .snm extension) in the new folders **(Figure 8.13)**.

6. Return to Netscape and open the Mail window. Voilà! Hierarchical, nested folders **(Figure 8.14)**.

Nesting folders

Importing messages from another folder

Netscape stores all the messages in each folder in a single file. You can copy these mail folder files between computers and then open them to access the messages they contain. You can also open the mail folder files in your own Mail window to copy the messages into a new folder, but I'm not quite sure why you'd want to.

To import messages from another folder:

1. Choose Open Folder in the File menu **(Figure 8.15)**. The Open dialog box appears.

2. Find and select the mail folder file that you wish to import and click Open **(Figure 8.16)**. The folder file is imported into the left pane of the Mail window **(Figure 8.17)**.

3. Click the folder file to see the messages it contains.

✔ Tips

■ Generally, mail folder files are stored in the Mail folder inside the Netscape folder, inside the Preferences folder, inside the System folder on the start-up disk. Don't use the files that end in .snm, but rather the ones with no extension.

■ If a folder already exists with the same name as the imported folder, the name of the new folder in the Mail window is the path to the selected mail folder file. To change the folder name, see the tip on the previous page.

Figure 8.15 *Choose Open Folder in the File menu.*

Figure 8.16 *Choose the desired folder file in the dialog box and click Open.*

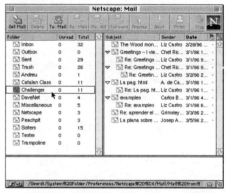

Figure 8.17 *The new folder appears in the left pane of the Mail window.*

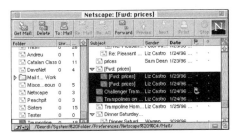

Figure 8.18 *Hold down Shift and click to select several messages in a row.*

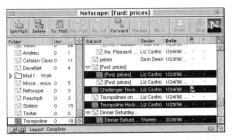

Figure 8.19 *Hold down Command and click to select several messages that are not in a row.*

Figure 8.20 *Choose Select Flagged Messages in the Edit menu.*

Figure 8.21 *All of the flagged messages in the current folder are selected.*

Selecting messages

There are several ways to select messages that make it easier to file, read, or delete a particular group of messages.

To select more than one message:

Hold down Shift and click to add one or more messages that are next to the currently selected message **(Figure 8.18)**. Hold down Command and click to add one or more messages that are not next to the currently selected one **(Figure 8.19)**.

You can also select all the flagged messages in a folder, perhaps prior to moving them to another folder en masse. For more information about flags, consult *Flagging messages* on page 99.

To select the flagged messages:

1. Select the desired folder.

2. Choose Select Flagged Messages in the Edit menu **(Figure 8.20)**. All of the flagged messages in the currently selected folder are selected **(Figure 8.21)**.

Selecting messages

You can also select all the messages in a thread (in a folder) in order to move, copy, or delete them at once. For more information about threads, consult *Threading messages* on page 101.

To select a thread:

1. Select the folder that contains the thread.

2. Choose Select Thread in the Edit menu **(Figure 8.22)**. Each message that belongs to the thread is selected **(Figure 8.23)**.

Last but not least, you can select all the messages in a folder.

To select all the messages in a folder:

1. Select the desired folder.

2. Choose Select All Messages (Command-A) in the Edit menu **(Fig. 8.24)**. All the messages in the chosen folder are selected **(Figure 8.25)**.

✔ Tips

■ You can't select messages in more than one folder at a time.

■ Once you've selected a group of messages, you can move or copy them to another folder, or delete them. For more information on moving and copying messages, consult *Moving and copying messages* on page 95. For more information on deleting messages, consult *Deleting messages and folders* on page 96.

Figure 8.22 *Choose Select Thread in the Edit menu.*

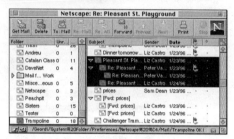

Figure 8.23 *All of the messages related to the original message—that is, in the message's thread—are selected.*

Figure 8.24 *Choose Select All in the Edit menu.*

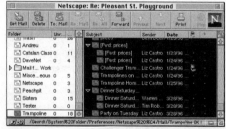

Figure 8.25 *All of the messages in the folder are selected.*

Selecting messages

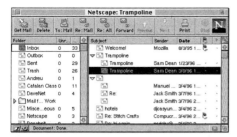

Figure 8.26 *Select the desired message.*

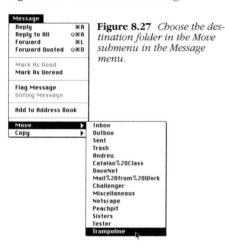

Figure 8.27 *Choose the destination folder in the Move submenu in the Message menu.*

Figure 8.28 *To copy a message, select it and then choose the destination folder in the Copy submenu in the Message menu.*

Moving and copying messages

Generally, in order to keep things organized, you move messages from Netscape's default folders (e.g., the Inbox and Sent folders) to the folders you have created. *Copying* moves the message to the new folder and leaves a copy in the old one.

To move messages to a different folder:

1. Select the message(s) **(Figure 8.26)**.

2. Choose the desired destination folder under Move in the Message menu **(Figure 8.27)**. The message disappears from the current folder and is transferred to the selected one.

To copy messages to a different folder:

1. Select the message(s).

2. Choose the desired destination folder under Copy in the Message menu **(Figure 8.28)**. The message remains in the current folder and is also copied to the selected one.

✔ Tips

■ You can also drag messages from one folder to another. Hold down Option while you drag to copy.

■ Use the special selecting commands *(see page 93)* to select more than one message before moving or copying.

■ You cannot move or copy messages to the Outbox folder. The only way to place messages there is by sending them with Deferred Delivery selected. For details, consult *Composing messages offline* on page 112.

Moving and copying messages

Deleting messages and folders

Once you no longer need a message, you can delete it in order to conserve space on your hard disk and keep your Mail window reasonably neat.

To delete a message:

1. Select the desired message(s) **(Figure 8.29)**.

2. Choose Delete Message from the Edit menu **(Figure 8.30)** or press Command-Delete. No alert box will appear to confirm the deletion. The message simply disappears from the current folder and is moved to the Trash folder **(Figure 8.31)**.

You can only delete a folder after you've deleted all the messages it contains.

To delete a folder:

1. Select the desired folder.

2. Choose Delete Folder in the Edit menu **(Figure 8.32)** or press Command Delete. No alert box will appear to confirm the deletion. The folder simply disappears forever.

✔ Tips

■ To recover a message you've deleted, simply drag it out of the Trash folder.

■ You can also drag a message to the Trash folder to delete it.

■ Press Command-Z immediately after deleting one or more messages or a folder to restore the items to their previous location.

Figure 8.29 *Choose the message you wish to delete.*

Figure 8.30 *Choose Delete Message in the Edit menu.*

Figure 8.31 *The message disappears from the current folder and is placed in the Trash.*

Figure 8.32 *To delete a folder, select it and then choose Delete Folder in the Edit menu.*

Figure 8.33 *To permanently remove the deleted messages, choose Empty Trash Folder in the File menu.*

Figure 8.34 *The Trash folder is empty.*

Figure 8.35 *Choose Compress Folder in the File menu.*

Conserving disk space

When you delete a message, it is not permanently deleted, but instead is placed in the Trash folder. You can retrieve an item from the Trash folder at any time before emptying it *(see page 95)*. Empty the trash to permanently remove the messages it contains.

To empty the Trash folder:

Choose Empty Trash Folder in the File menu **(Figure 8.33)**. No alert box appears, nor will the Undo command make your messages come back. The Trash folder simply appears empty **(Figure 8.34)**.

Another way to reduce the amount of space taken up by your folders and messages is by compressing your folders.

To compress a folder:

1. Select the folder you wish to compress.

2. Choose Compress Folder in the File menu **(Figure 8.35)**. The folder is compressed.

✔ Tips

- ■ The amount of space you can recover by compressing a folder is shown in the status area of the Mail window when the folder is selected.

- ■ Emptying the trash automatically compresses all the folders.

- ■ Compressing a folder does not affect any of the messages it contains. It simply recovers wasted space that is generated when you move messages from one folder to another.

Conserving disk space

Putting your messages in order

You can view your messages in order of Date, Subject, or Sender, or even by Message Number. They may be sorted in ascending or descending order, although the latter is the default option. Mail folders (and newsgroups) are always displayed in alphabetical order.

To put your messages in order:

1. Select By Date, By Subject, By Sender, or By Message Number under Sort View menu **(Figure 8.36)**. The messages are sorted according to the criteria chosen.

2. Toggle the Ascending option under Sort in the View menu to list the letters in ascending (when the option is checked) or descending order **(Figure 8.37)**.

✔ Tips

■ You can also click the column heading (Sender, Subject, or Date) to sort your messages by the contents of that column **(Figure 8.38, Figure 8.39, and Figure 8.40)**. To sort by Message number, you have to use the menu.

■ The header of the column by which the messages are sorted appears in boldface.

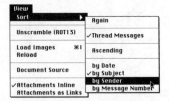

Figure 8.36 *Choose By Sender under Sort in the View menu to put the messages in order by sender.*

Figure 8.37 *Choose Ascending under Sort in the View menu to choose the direction in which to sort.*

Figure 8.38 *Descending order, by sender.*

Figure 8.39 *Descending order by Subject. Notice that* Re: *is ignored.*

Figure 8.40 *Descending order, by date.*

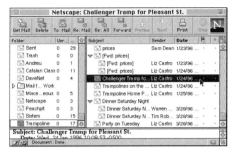

Figure 8.41 *Select the message you wish to flag.*

Figure 8.42 *Choose Flag Message in the Message menu.*

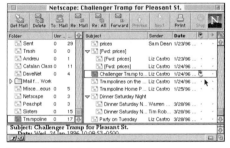

Figure 8.43 *A little red flag appears next to the message.*

Flagging messages

In a busy mailbox, it's sometimes hard to keep your eye on an important piece of mail. One easy way to make a message stand out is to mark or flag it.

To flag or unflag a message:

1. Select the desired message in the right pane of the Mail window **(Fig. 8.41)**.

2. Choose Flag Message in the Message window **(Figure 8.42)**. A checkmark next to the command indicates that the message is flagged. Choose the command again to toggle it. A little red flag appears in the Flagged column next to the flagged message **(Figure 8.43)**. The flag disappears when you unflag the message.

✔ Tips

■ You can flag a message (or remove its flag) by clicking in the Flagged column next to the desired message.

■ You can navigate through only the flagged messages using the First Flagged, Next Flagged, and Previous Flagged commands in the Go menu. For more information on getting from message to message, consult *Navigating through your messages* on page 108.

Flagging messages

99

Marking mail as read or unread

When you receive new mail, Netscape marks it with a green diamond so that you know that it's new. Once you've read a message, the mark disappears. You can choose to restore the Unread mark to remind yourself to return to that message at a later date. You can also mark mail as read, even if you haven't read it—perhaps because you can tell from the Subject line that the message is not of interest to you.

To mark mail as read or unread:

1. Select the desired messages in the Mail window's right pane **(Fig. 8.44)**.

2. In the Message menu, choose Mark as Unread or Mark as Read **(Fig. 8.45)**. A green diamond appears next to messages that are unread and disappears for messages that you've read or marked as read **(Figure 8.46)**.

✔ Tips

■ You can also mark a message as read or unread by clicking in the Read column (the one with the green diamond) next to the desired message.

■ You can navigate through the unread messages using the First Unread, Next Unread, and Previous Unread commands in the Go menu. For more information about navigating, consult *Navigating through your messages* on page 108.

■ You can mark a single message as read without opening it (which automatically marks it as read). The trick is to click right on the diamond, not on the title of the message.

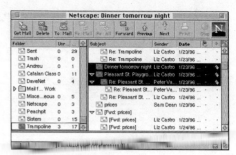

Figure 8.44 *Choose the unread messages that you wish to mark as read.*

Figure 8.45 *Choose Mark as Read in the Message menu.*

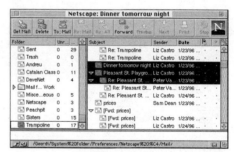

Figure 8.46 *The newly "read" messages appear in plain text and the green diamonds disappear.*

Marking mail as read or unread

Figure 8.47 *Unthreaded messages appear independently in the Mail window's right pane.*

Figure 8.48 *Choose Thread Messages under Sort in the View menu to relate messages with similar subjects.*

Figure 8.49 *Threaded messages appear in hierarchical form with the original message at the top and replies below and to the right.*

Figure 8.50 *Click the triangle to the left of the original message's letter icon to hide the replies. Click it again to reveal the replies.*

Figure 8.51 *Click on the Thread icon to thread or unthread the messages.*

Thread icon

Threading messages

Netscape can relate all the replies (and replies to replies) that are generated from a single original message into a wonderful invention called a *thread*. This makes it easy to follow a particular conversation from start to finish even if you have a busy mailbox. You can choose to view your e-mail in threads, or as individual messages.

To thread messages:

1. Choose Thread Messages under Sort in the View menu **(Figure 8.48)**. The option will have a check next to it when it is active. Choose the option again to toggle it. Each message that is related to another will appear underneath the parent message **(Fig. 8.49)**.

2. Click the triangle next to a threaded message group to hide the replies beneath it. Click the triangle again to reveal the replies beneath it **(Figure 8.50)**.

✔ Tip

■ Click the icon above the scroll bar to the right of the upper right pane to toggle the Thread Messages option **(Figure 8.51)**.

Threading messages

101

Changing the size of the panes

You can change the size of each of the three panes, according to the task at hand. For example, if you're filing mail, you'll want the two upper panes as large as possible **(Figure 8.54)**. On the other hand, if you're reading a series of messages, it will be better to make the lower pane as large as possible **(Figure 8.55)**.

To change the size of the panes:

1. Place the pointer over one of the separators between the panes **(Figure 8.52)**.

2. Click with the mouse and drag to make the panes larger or smaller **(Figure 8.53, Figure 8.54, and Figure 8.55)**.

✔ Tips

■ You can resize the entire window by dragging in the usual way.

■ If you make the panes so short that not all the contents can be seen at once, scroll bars will appear to let you get to the hidden items. This does not happen if you make a pane too narrow; in that case, the hidden material stays out of sight.

■ If you make the window too short to see the bottom pane, you won't be able to see the contents of your messages, and scrolling won't help.

■ When you change the width of the panes, either by moving the pane separator as described above or by changing the window size, the width of the *columns* is not affected. For more information, consult *Changing the columns* on page 103.

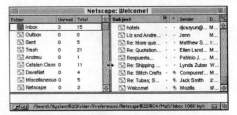

Figure 8.52 *To reduce the amount of wasted space in the left pane, place the pointer on the pane's border, click and drag to resize.*

Figure 8.53 *Now there is additional room in the right pane to display more information.*

Figure 8.54 *Drag the middle border to the bottom to hide the contents of messages (and have more room for folder and message titles).*

Figure 8.55 *Drag the middle border to the top to hide the folders and message titles and thus have more space for the message itself.*

Figure 8.56 *Some of the Subject titles are cut off. To make the Subject column wider, click the right border of the column and drag to resize.*

Figure 8.57 *Once the column is wider, you can see more of the titles.*

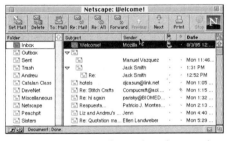

Figure 8.58 *To move the Sender column to the left of the Subject column, simply click the Sender header and drag it to the left of the Subject header.*

Changing the columns

There is a lot of information jammed into eight columns between two panes in the Mail (and News) window. You can adjust the width or order of the columns to suit your particular task.

To change the column width:

1. Place the cursor on the left border of the column's title **(Figure 8.56)**.

2. Drag to adjust the size of the column **(Figure 8.57)**.

You may find it easier to organize your messages if the columns are arranged in a special order. For example, you could put the Marked and Read columns to the left of the Sender column.

To change the column order:

Click in the desired column's title and drag it to the new position **(Figure 8.58)**. The other columns are adjusted accordingly.

✔ **Tip**

■ If you aren't interested in a particular column's data, drag it to the rightmost position in the pane. Then, either make the other columns larger or the pane or window smaller so that the undesired columns are hidden from view.

Changing the columns

Changing your messages' appearance

You can change the appearance of messages in the Mail (and News) window to make them easier to read.

To change your messages' appearance:

1. Choose Mail and News Preferences in the Options menu **(Figure 8.59)**. The Mail and News Preferences window appears.

2. Click the Appearance tab at the top left corner of the window to show the Appearance preferences **(Fig. 8.60)**.

3. In the first section, choose Fixed Width Font to show your messages in a font like Courier or Variable Width Font to show your messages in a font like Times or Helvetica.

4. In the second section, choose a style and a size for the quoted text in your messages.

5. Click OK to close the Preferences window. The messages in the Mail (and News) window will now appear with the type of font selected. Quotes will appear with the style selected **(Figure 8.61)**.

✔ Tips

- You can specify the actual fonts in the Fonts tab of the General Preferences dialog box *(see page 160)*.

- Unfortunately, these options have no effect on the Message Composition window (where they would be particularly handy).

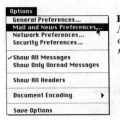

Figure 8.59 *Choose Mail and News Preferences in the Options menu.*

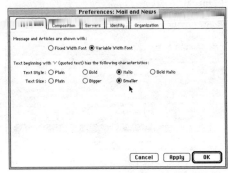

Figure 8.60 *Click the Appearance tab at the top left corner of the window to show the Appearances preferences. Then choose the desired font type and style.*

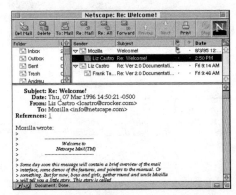

Figure 8.61 *Notice how the entire note is displayed in a Variable Width Font (Times, in this case) and that the quoted part of the note is in italics.*

Reading and Sending Mail

Figure 9.1 *Click the letter icon in the lower right corner of the Netscape window to retrieve your mail from the server.*

Figure 9.2 *Another way to retrieve your mail is by choosing Get New Mail in the Mail window's File menu.*

Figure 9.3 *Last but not least, you can also click the Get Mail button at the left of the toolbar to check your mail.*

Figure 9.4 *Regardless of the method you choose, Netscape places new mail in the Inbox, and indicates new, unread messages with a green diamond.*

You can use Netscape to compose and send new mail, or to read or reply to mail that you've received from others.

Getting new mail

Once you have a new e-mail address, checking to see if someone has actually sent you something becomes almost an obsession. Luckily, Netscape gives you several ways to check your electronic mailbox.

To get new mail from the browser or News window:

Click the letter icon in the bottom right corner of the screen **(Figure 9.1)**. Netscape will open the Mail window, ask for your password if necessary *(see page 88)*, consult your server, and finally show you your new mail (if you have any).

If you've already opened the Mail window, you can click the mail icon or choose the command from the menu.

To get new mail from the Mail window:

Choose Get New Mail in the File menu **(Figure 9.2)**. The new mail, if any, will be displayed in the Inbox folder **(Figure 9.4)**.

✔ Tip

■ You can also click the Get Mail button on the Mail window's toolbar to get mail **(Figure 9.3)**.

Having Netscape check for mail periodically

When you are connected to the Internet, you can have Netscape check for mail every few minutes all on its own and alert you when you've received something. Obviously, if you're not connected, Netscape won't be able to tell if you have mail.

To have Netscape check for mail periodically:

1. Choose Mail and News Preferences in the Options menu **(Figure 9.5)**. The Preferences dialog box appears.

2. Click the Servers tab at the top of the dialog box **(Figure 9.6)**.

3. At the bottom of the Mail section, click the radio button next to Check for mail every and enter a number to determine how often Netscape will check the server for mail.

4. Click OK to close the Preferences dialog box.

✔ Tips

■ Netscape doesn't automatically copy mail from the server—it just checks to see if there is any. If there is, it notifies you with an exclamation point next to the letter icon **(Figure 9.7)**. You still have to *get* your mail *(see page 105)*.

■ If you don't want Netscape constantly checking for mail, choose Never in step 3.

■ Netscape will only check for mail automatically if you have saved your mail password *(see page 88)*.

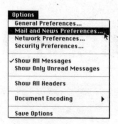

Figure 9.5 *Choose Mail and News Preferences from the Options menu.*

Figure 9.6 *First click Servers at the top of the dialog box. Then click the radio button next to Check for mail every and type a number in the minutes box.*

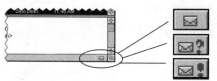

Figure 9.7 *A plain letter icon means you have no letters waiting on the server. A question mark means Netscape can't tell if you have any mail waiting (you're probably not connected). An exclamation point means someone has sent you something!*

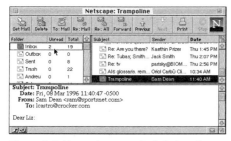

Figure 9.8 *To read new mail, click the Inbox in the left pane. To read filed mail, click a different folder. Then click a message title in the right pane to open it.*

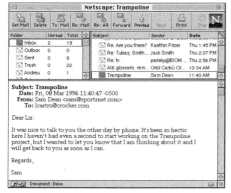

Figure 9.9 *The message is displayed in the lower pane of the Mail window. (I've also made the entire Mail window larger here, in order to see all three panes.)*

Figure 9.10 *To hide all but the unread messages in the upper right pane of the Mail window, choose Show Only Unread Messages in the Options menu.*

Figure 9.11 *To show a message's additional information, choose Show All Headers in the Options menu.*

Reading mail

Once you have received new mail, you can open it and read it. You can also re-read mail received earlier, or read mail that you have sent to others.

To read mail:

1. Click the folder in the top left pane that contains the e-mail you want to read **(Figure 9.8)**. You'll find new mail in the Inbox folder. The contents of the folder appear in the top right pane.

2. Click the message that you want to read. The contents of the message appear in the bottom pane of the window **(Figure 9.9)**.

3. Use the scroll bars in the lower pane to move around in the note.

✔ Tips

■ You can have the Mail window display only those messages that you haven't read yet by choosing Show Only Unread Messages in the Options menu **(Figure 9.10)**.

■ You can show additional information about a message, including the route it took to get to you (which is sometimes useful for exposing fraudulent messages), by choosing Show All Headers in the Options menu **(Figure 9.11)**.

■ Thankfully, the Mail window can be rearranged according to the task at hand. When reading, make the bottom pane as large as possible. When filing, make the upper panes larger. For more information on changing the panes, consult *Changing the size of the panes* on page 102.

Reading mail

Navigating through your messages

Netscape's Go menu makes it easy to move from one message to the next.

To open the next message:

Choose Next Message in the Go menu or press the down arrow **(Figure 9.12)**.

To open the previous message:

Choose Previous Message in the Go menu or press the up arrow.

✔ Tips

- ■ The up and down arrows only work if the cursor is in the upper-right pane of the window. If you've clicked in the lower pane, the up and down arrows simply navigate you through that particular message.

- ■ You can jump to the first unread message by choosing First Unread in the Go menu. Jump to the next and previous unread messages by choosing Next Unread and Previous Unread, respectively **(Figure 9.13)**. (*Next* in this case means *below* the current message. *Previous* means *above* the current message, and does not refer to the unread message you read before the current one.) For more information, consult *Marking mail as read or unread* on page 100.

- ■ Jump to the first flagged message by choosing First Flagged in the Go menu **(Figure 9.14)**. Jump to the next and previous flagged messages by choosing Next Flagged and Previous Flagged. For more information, consult *Flagging messages* on page 99.

Figure 9.12 *Click Next Message or Previous Message in the Go menu to move from one message to another.*

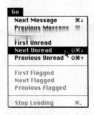

Figure 9.13 *Choose any of the [illegible] commands (First Unread, Next Unread, or Previous Unread) to navigate only among those messages that you have not read.*

Figure 9.14 *Choose First, Next, or Previous Flagged to navigate among the marked messages.*

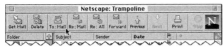

Figure 9.15 *Choose New Mail Message in the File menu to start a new e-mail message.*

Figure 9.16 *You can also click the To: Mail button on the toolbar to start a new message.*

Figure 9.17 *In the Message Composition window, type the recipient's address in the Mail To field, type a Subject, add an Attachment (if desired) and type the contents of the message.*

Figure 9.18 *Once you're satisfied with the message, choose Send Mail Now in the File menu. (For deferred delivery, consult Composing messages offline on page 112.)*

Figure 9.19 *You can also send a finished message by clicking the Send Now button at the top left of the Message Composition window.*

Composing a new message

Somehow, e-mail is a thousand times easier to write than a conventional letter.

To compose a new message:

1. Choose New Mail Message in the File menu **(Figure 9.15)** or click the To: Mail button **(Fig. 9.16)**. A fresh Message Composition window appears.

2. Type the recipient's address in the Mail To field. Separate multiple addresses with a comma **(Fig. 9.17)**.

3. Type the address(es) where you wish to send "carbon" copies in the Cc box.

4. Type a subject for the message. The subject is important; as the most visible part of the message, it is often used as the criteria for filing.

5. Click the Attachment button to attach a file or URL to the message *(see page 120)*.

6. Type the contents of the message in the area at the bottom of the window.

7. Choose Send Mail Now in the File menu or click the Send Now (or Send Later) button to send the message **(Figure 9.18 and Figure 9.19)** .

✔ Tips

■ Click the Address button to make the Address book appear.

■ By default, your messages are sent immediately. For information on deferred sending, consult *Composing messages offline* on page 112.

■ Double click a name in the Address book to open a new message automatically addressed to that person.

Composing a new message

Viewing or hiding the parts of a message

A message can have up to nine sections: From, Reply To, Mail To, Mail Cc, Mail Bcc, Newsgroups, Followups To, Subject, and Attachment. You can show or hide any combination of these message parts.

To view or hide parts of a message:

1. Choose New Mail Message in the File menu to open the Message Composition window **(Figure 9.20)**. By default, you'll see the Subject, Mail To, Cc, and Attachment fields **(Figure 9.21)**.

2. Choose the desired message part from the View menu **(Figure 9.22)**. When the option has a checkmark, that message part will be visible. You can also choose Show All in the View menu to view all nine message parts.

✔ Tips

■ Click the triangle next to Addressing to hide or show all the addressing parts of the message. Only the parts selected in the View menu will appear or disappear.

■ Some of the message parts are self explanatory. Others are not so clear. *From* is your e-mail address. *Reply To* is the address where replies should be sent. *Mail Cc* is for sending a "carbon" copy of the message to others. *Mail Bcc* is for sending a copy to others without the recipient knowing. *Newsgroups* shows the newsgroup to which you wish to post the message *(see page 150)*.

Figure 9.20 *Choose New Mail Message in the File menu to open the Message Composition window.*

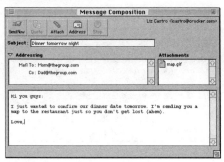

Figure 9.21 *By default, the Message Composition window shows the Mail To, Cc, Subject, and Attachment fields, as well as the contents.*

Figure 9.22 *Choose the message part that you wish to see in the View menu. Visible parts are shown with a checkmark. (Choose a checked item to uncheck it and hide it in the Message Composition window.)*

Figure 9.23 *After choosing Reply To in the View menu, the corresponding field is displayed in the Message Composition window.*

110

Figure 9.24 *Select a message.*

Figure 9.25 *Choose Reply or Reply to All in the Mail window's Message menu.*

Figure 9.26 *You can also click the Reply button.*

Figure 9.27 *The Mail To and Subject fields are automatically filled in and the contents may contain a quoted version of the original message.*

Figure 9.28 *Type the new material and Send.*

Replying to a message you've received

Replying to someone else's message instead of creating a new message *(see page 109)* has certain advantages: the addressing is done automatically and you can choose to quote the original letter in your reply.

To reply to a message you've received:

1. Select the message to which you wish to reply **(Figure 9.24)**.

2. Choose Reply in the Message window **(Figure 9.25)** or click the Re: Mail button on the toolbar **(Figure 9.26)**. The Message Composition window appears. The Mail To box is automatically filled in. The original letter may or may not be quoted in the message area *(see page 115)*. The subject area contains the original subject preceded by "Re:" **(Figure 9.27)**.

3. Type the body of the message **(Figure 9.28)**.

4. Click the Send button or choose the Send command in the File menu *(see page 109)*. Unless you have chosen Deferred Delivery in the Options menu *(see page 112)*, your reply is sent immediately.

✔ Tip

■ If the original message was addressed to more than one person, you can reply to all of them at once by selecting Reply to All in the Message menu, or by clicking Re: All on the toolbar.

Replying to a message you've received

Composing messages offline

If you have a dial-up Internet connection, you can compose messages offline and then send them all together once you've connected. Not only does this save a lot of money, but it'll let you relax as you write.

To compose messages offline:

1. Disconnect from the Internet without quitting Netscape (or launch Netscape without connecting to the Internet).

2. Choose New Mail Message in the File menu or select a message and choose Reply in the Message menu **(Figure 9.29)**. The Message Composition window appears.

3. In the Message Composition window's Options menu, choose Deferred Delivery **(Figure 9.30)**.

4. Compose the message as usual (see page 109).

5. Choose Send Mail Later in the File menu or click the Send Later button in the Message Composition window **(Figure 9.31 and Figure 9.32)**. The message is stored in the Outbox.

6. When you're ready to send the message(s) consult *Sending the messages in the Outbox* on page 113.

✔ Tips

■ To return to immediate sending, open the Message Composition window and choose Immediate delivery in the Options menu.

■ If you change your mind about sending a message in the Outbox, simply drag it to another folder (see page 90) or delete it (see page 96).

Figure 9.29 *Either choose New Mail Message in the File menu, or select a message and choose Reply or Reply to All in the Message menu.*

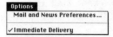

Figure 9.30 *Choose Deferred Delivery in the Message Composition's Options menu to hold off sending your messages until later (presumably when you've connected up again).*

Figure 9.31 *When you've finished composing your message, choose Send Mail Later in the File menu.*

Figure 9.32 *You can also click the Send Later button on the toolbar.*

Composing messages offline

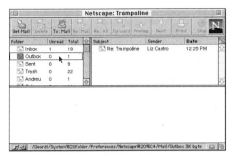

Figure 9.33 *As you compose messages offline and "send" them as described on page 112, they are stored in the Outbox folder.*

Figure 9.34 *Once you've connected to the Internet and are ready to send your messages, choose Send Mail in Outbox in the File menu.*

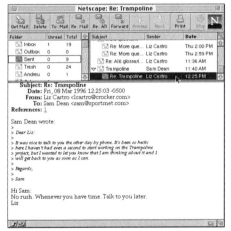

Figure 9.35 *Once you send the messages in the Outbox, they are moved from the Outbox folder to the Sent folder.*

Sending the messages in the Outbox

If you've composed several messages offline—both e-mail and news *(see page 153)*—you can choose to send them when it is convenient for you.

To send the messages in the Outbox:

1. If desired, click the Outbox in the Mail window to see which messages you've stored for later delivery **(Figure 9.33)**.

2. Open your Internet connection.

3. With the Mail window active, choose Send Mail in Outbox in the File menu **(Figure 9.34)**. All your stored mail and news postings are sent. Netscape automatically transfers sent messages to the Sent folder **(Figure 9.35)**. For more information on the Sent folder, consult *The Mail window's four default folders* on page 89.

4. Close your Internet connection, if desired.

✔ Tip

■ If the Send Mail in Outbox option does not appear, make sure the Mail window is open and active.

Sending the messages in the Outbox

Editing messages in the Outbox

Unfortunately, it's not as easy as it should be to edit a message once you've stored it in the Outbox for deferred delivery *(see page 112)*. However, you can leave Netscape and use any text editor or word processor to do the trick.

To edit a message in the Outbox:

1. Close the Mail window.

2. Open any text editor.

3. Choose Open in the text editor's File menu **(Figure 9.37)**.

4. Select the Outbox file, which you'll find in the Mail folder, inside the Netscape folder, in the Preferences folder, in the System folder, on your hard disk **(Figure 9.38)**.

5. Edit the document **(Figure 9.39)**.

6. Save the document. Be sure to save the file in Text Only format. Do not change its name.

7. Return to Netscape and open the Mail window. Click the Outbox folder and then click the message to review the changes **(Figure 9.40)**.

✔ Tip

- If you change your mind about sending a message that you've stored in the Outbox for deferred delivery, you can move *(see page 95)* or delete the message *(see page 96)* so that it does not reach the recipient. Of course, you have to do this before actually sending the message.

Figure 9.36 *The original message in the Outbox.*

Figure 9.37 *Choose Open in the text editor or word processor's File menu. (This is SimpleText.)*

Figure 9.38 *Open the Outbox file in the Mail folder, which you'll find in the Netscape folder.*

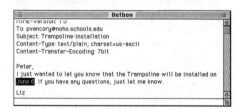
Figure 9.39 *In the open Outbox file, make any necessary corrections. You may have to scroll to the message you wish to edit. (The Outbox file contains all the outgoing messages.)*

Figure 9.40 *Return to Netscape and open the message in the Outbox to review the changes (the date, in this example).*

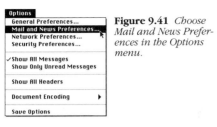

Figure 9.41 *Choose Mail and News Preferences in the Options menu.*

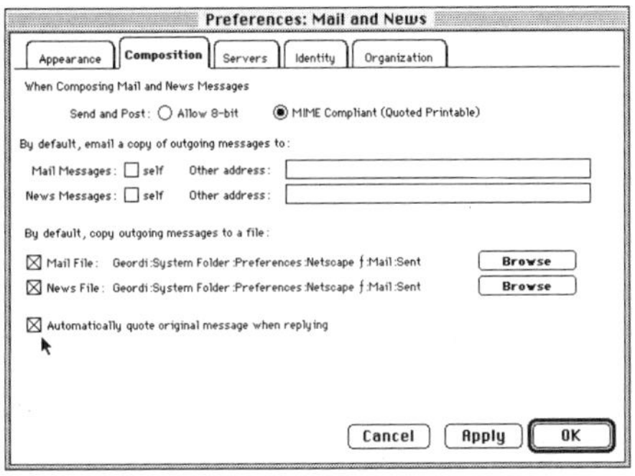

Figure 9.42 *Click the Composition tab and then check Automatically quote original message when replying at the bottom of the window.*

Quoting every message

When you reply to a message, you can have Netscape automatically "quote" the original correspondence, so that the recipient readily knows what you are responding to. Each line of a quoted message is preceded with a greater than sign (>), by Internet convention, and the original author's name is inserted at the beginning of the quote.

To quote every message:

1. Choose Mail and News Preferences in the Options menu **(Figure 9.41)**. The Preferences dialog box appears.

2. Click the Composition tab at the top of the window. The Composition preferences appear **(Figure 9.42)**.

3. Mark the option Automatically quote original message when replying at the bottom of the dialog box. Leave the option unchecked if you don't want Netscape to include a copy of the original message every time you reply.

4. Click OK to close the Preferences dialog box. From now on, each message you reply to will automatically include a copy of the original message.

✔ Tip

■ You can choose how the quoted material appears in the Mail window (although not in the Message Composition window). For more details, consult *Changing your messages' appearance* on page 104.

Quoting individual messages

Having Netscape quote every message you reply to can get a little tiresome, especially if the original messages are often long. You can turn off Netscape's automatic quoting and then quote messages individually, when desired.

To quote individual messages:

1. Generally, you will have turned Netscape's automatic feature off, as described on page 115, unchecking the option in step 3 **(Figure 9.43)**.

2. Reply to a message in the normal way **(Figure 9.44 and Figure 9.45)**. See page 111 for details. The Message Composition window appears.

3. In the Message Composition window click the Quote button **(Fig. 9.46)** or choose Include Original Text in the File menu **(Figure 9.47)**. The original message appears in the message area, labeled with the original author's name. Each line of a quote is preceded by greater than signs (>), as is the convention on the Internet **(Figure 9.48)**.

4. You may cut out parts of the quote if you don't wish to quote the entire original message. Simply select them with the mouse and choose Cut from the Edit menu, or press Delete.

✔ Tip

■ You can change the way a quote is displayed in the Mail window, but unfortunately, not in the Message Composition window. For more details, consult *Changing your messages' appearance* on page 104.

Figure 9.43 *Uncheck the Automatically quote original messages when replying option in the Composition preferences dialog box (cf Figure 9.42).*

Figure 9.44 *Choose Reply or Reply to All in the Message menu.*

Figure 9.45 *Or click the Re: Mail or Re: All buttons on the toolbar.*

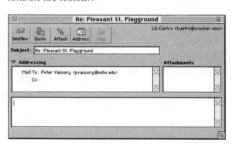

Figure 9.46 *The Mail To and Subject fields are automatically filled in. Click the Quote button to quote the original message.*

Figure 9.47 *Or choose Include Original Text in the File menu.*

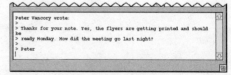

Figure 9.48 *The original message is quoted at the bottom of the Message Composition window.*

Quoting individual messages

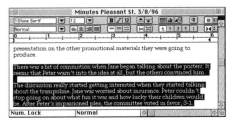

Figure 9.49 *Select the material that you wish to quote in the original document. (This is from Word.)*

Figure 9.50 *Choose Copy (again, this is Word) to copy the material to the clipboard.*

Figure 9.51 *Switch back to the Message Composition window in Netscape and choose Paste as Quotation in the Edit menu.*

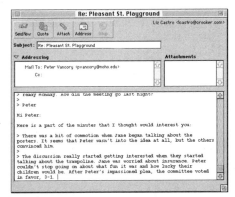

Figure 9.52 *The copied material is pasted in the contents area with a greater than sign (>) at the beginning of each line (well, paragraph).*

Custom quoting

If you don't want to quote the entire message, or if you want to quote several parts of various messages, you can use Netscape's custom quoting feature to add greater than signs at the beginning of each line of text.

To quote a part of a message:

1. Select the text that you wish to quote **(Figure 9.49)**. The text may be from any file; it doesn't have to be from a message received with Netscape.

2. Choose Copy (Command-C) in the Edit menu **(Figure 9.50)**.

3. With the Message Composition window active in Netscape, choose Paste as Quotation in the Edit menu **(Fig. 9.51)**. The copied text will be pasted with a greater than sign at the beginning of each line **(Fig. 9.52)**.

✔ Tip

■ Netscape actually inserts a greater than sign (the Internet-recognized symbol for quoted text) at the beginning of each *paragraph*. Since most electronic mail is made up of one-line paragraphs, this system works fine for quoting from messages. If you paste text from other programs, you may notice that there is only one greater than sign at the beginning of each paragraph. In this case, either insert the additional symbols manually, or copy each line individually.

Forwarding a message

Sometimes you will receive e-mail that either isn't for you or that you would like to share with others. The easiest way to share mail you have received with other people is to forward it.

To forward a message as an attachment:

1. Select the message that you wish to forward in the Mail window **(Figure 9.53)**. The contents of the message appear in the lower pane.

2. Select Forward in the Message menu **(Figure 9.54)**. The Message Composition window appears. The Subject is automatically set to "[Fwd: title of original message]" and the original message is attached to the new message.

3. Enter the recipient's address in the Mail To box.

4. Fill in the other message parts as desired.

5. Add any personal comments about the forwarded material in the message area.

6. Click the Send button or choose the Send command in the File menu.

✔ Tips

■ You can also click the Forward button on the toolbar to forward a message **(Figure 9.55)**

■ A forwarded message appears below the main message, much like an attached document **(Figure 9.56)**.

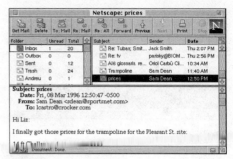

Figure 9.53 *Choose the message you wish to forward.*

Figure 9.54 *Choose Forward in the Message menu.*

Figure 9.55 *Or, click the Forward button.*

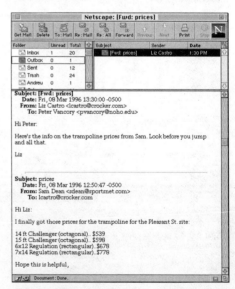

Figure 9.56 *A forwarded message appears below the new portion of the current message.*

Figure 9.57 *Choose the message that you wish to forward.*

Figure 9.58 *Choose Forward Quoted in the Message menu.*

Figure 9.59 *The forwarded message appears as a quote (with >) in the contents area.*

Figure 9.60 *Type the new material below the quoted message.*

Forwarding a message as a quote

You can also forward a message as a quote.

To forward a message as a quote:

1. Select the message that you wish to forward in the Mail window **(Figure 9.57)**. The contents of the message appear in the lower pane.

2. Select Forward Quoted in the Message menu **(Figure 9.58)**. The Message Composition window appears. The Subject is automatically set to "[Fwd: title of original message]" and the original message is quoted in the message area **(Figure 9.59)**.

3. Enter the recipient's address in the Mail To box.

4. Fill in the other message parts as desired.

5. Add any personal comments about the forwarded material in the message area below the quoted, forwarded message **(Figure 9.60)**.

6. Click the Send button, or choose the Send command in the File menu.

Forwarding a message as a quote

Attaching files to a message

Electronic mail does not limit you to letters; you can send packages, too. You can attach any kind of file to a message—including images or even programs. You can also attach a URL to a message, giving the recipient direct access to a Web page (*see page 121*).

To attach a file to a message:

1. Choose New Mail Message in the File menu or select a message and choose Reply in the Message menu. The Message Composition window appears.

2. Choose Attach in the File menu **(Figure 9.61)** or click the Attachment field button.

3. In the Attachments dialog box that appears, click Attach File **(Fig. 9.62)**.

4. In the dialog box that appears, select the file that you wish to send with the message and click Open **(Fig. 9.63)**.

5. Back in the Attachments dialog box, choose Source to send the file in its current form or choose Plain Text to send the file as text **(Figure 9.64)**.

6. Click Done. The file's path appears in the Attachments box in the Message Composition window **(Fig. 9.65)**.

7. Compose the rest of the message.

✔ Tips

■ Click the Attachment field button to add or edit an attached file.

■ You can drag any file from the Finder and drop it in the Attachments box in the Message Composition window.

Figure 9.61 *Choose Attach in the File menu.*

Figure 9.62 *Click the Attach File button in the Attachments dialog box.*

Figure 9.63 *Choose the desired file and click Open.*

Figure 9.64 *The selected file appears in the Attachments dialog box. Click Source or Plain Text and then click Done.*

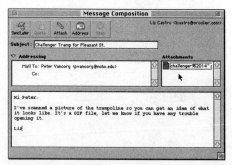

Figure 9.65 *The attached file appears in the Attachment field in the Message Composition window.*

Figure 9.66 *Click Attach Location (URL) in the Attachments dialog box.*

Figure 9.67 *Type or paste the URL (or use the current one, which is automatically entered from the last browser open) and click OK.*

Figure 9.68 *The URL appears in the Attachments dialog box. Click Source to send it with HTML tags and Plain Text to send it without.*

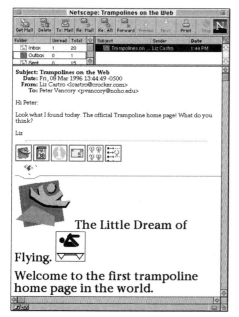

Figure 9.69 *As long as the recipient views the message with Netscape, the URL appears within the message just like a regular Web page.*

Attaching a URL to a message

If you find a great Web page on the Net and want to share it with someone, instead of sending the page's address in text form, you can send them the actual page within your message. As long as they use Netscape to view your message, the page will appear just as if they had jumped to it themselves.

To attach a URL to a message:

1. From the Message Composition window, choose Attach File or click the Attach button.

2. In the Attachments dialog that appears, click Attach Location (URL) **(Figure 9.66)**.

3. Type or paste the desired URL in the dialog box that appears and click OK **(Figure 9.67)**.

4. In the Attachments dialog box, choose Source to send the page with HTML tags; choose Plain Text to send it without **(Figure 9.68)**. For more information about tags, consult *Saving a Web page* on page 46.

5. Click Done to close the dialog box. The URL appears in the Attachments box in the Message Composition window.

6. Compose the rest of the message as usual (*see page 109*).

✔ Tips

■ Browse to the page you wish to send before clicking Attach. The URL will be automatically entered in the box.

■ If you're not sure what program the recipient uses for e-mail, send the page without tags.

Attaching a URL to a message

121

Mailing a document

Earlier versions of Netscape allowed you to mail a Web page directly from the browser. Although Netscape's mail features have expanded, the old command remains. The effect is virtually identical to attaching a URL *(see page 121)*. The only difference is that the actual URL, as a link, is added to the note above the page itself.

To mail a document:

1. In the browser, jump to or open the desired Web page.

2. Choose Mail Document in the File menu **(Figure 9.70)**. The Message Composition window appears with the Web page automatically attached and the URL as a link in the body of the message **(Figure 9.71)**.

3. Edit and send the message as usual *(see page 109)*. The mailed document appears both as a link and as an attachment to the recipient **(Figure 9.72)**.

✔ Tip

■ You can also mail an individual frame. Simply select the frame and the Mail Document command turns into Mail Frame in the File menu.

Figure 9.70 *Jump to (or open) the desired page and select Mail Document in the File menu.*

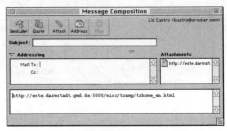

Figure 9.71 *The page's URL is attached and added to the contents of the message. Add the name and contents and send as usual.*

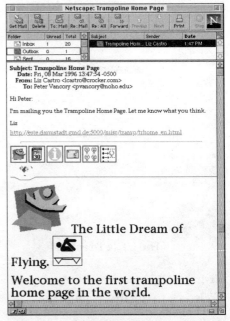

Figure 9.72 *The link to the page and the page itself appear below the message.*

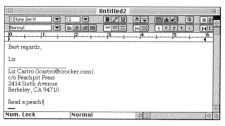

Figure 9.73 *A signature typically contains your name, e-mail, and snail mail addresses, and a pithy quote. This one was created with Word.*

Figure 9.74 *Choose Save As in the word processor's File menu.*

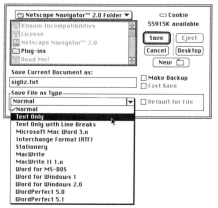

Figure 9.75 *Save the signature file in Text Only format.*

Creating a signature file

One of the nice traditions of e-mail writing is adding a few lines at the bottom of the note that tell who you are, and sometimes what you do and where you're from. You can create a signature in any word processor, including Simple Text or TeachText.

To create a signature:

1. Open a word processor or text editor. SimpleText is fine.

2. Create your signature as desired **(Figure 9.73)**. A signature typically contains your name, e-mail and snail mail addresses, and a pithy quote. You can also add ASCII images.

3. Choose Save As in the text editor's File menu **(Figure 9.74)**.

4. Give the file a name and choose the Text (*.TXT) format in the Save As dialog box **(Figure 9.75)**. Click Save.

5. To use the signature file, consult *Using a signature file* on page 124.

✔ Tip

■ Although a signature is limited to text characters, you can be creative about how to use them. Some people even make pictures out of text characters, or more simply, add famous quotes and sayings to their signatures.

Using a signature file

Once you've created a signature file *(see page 123)*, Netscape can automatically add it to each message that you send. All you have to do is tell Netscape where the signature file is.

To use a signature file:

1. In Netscape, choose Mail and News Preferences in the Options menu **(Figure 9.76)**.

2. In the Preferences dialog box that appears, click the Identity tab **(Figure 9.77)**.

3. At the bottom of the Identity preferences tab, click Browse.

4. Choose the desired signature file in the dialog box that appears and click Open **(Figure 9.78)**. The file's path will appear in the Identity preferences tab **(Figure 9.79)**.

5. Click OK to close the Identity tab. The next time you write a message, Netscape will include your signature automatically **(Figure 9.80)**.

✔ Tips

■ If the signature file does not appear in the Open dialog box when you try to choose it, you probably didn't save it in Text Only (or ASCII) format *(see page 123)*.

■ If you move the signature file, or change its name or the name of the folder it's in, Netscape won't be able to find it and will simply stop adding it to your messages. Unfortunately, Netscape won't tell you there's a problem, so you have to watch it.

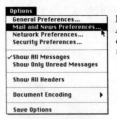

Figure 9.76 *Choose Mail and News Preferences in the Options menu.*

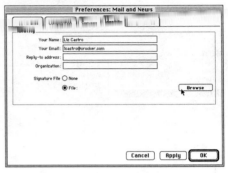

Figure 9.77 *Click the Identity tab and then the Browse button to choose a signature file.*

Figure 9.78 *Choose the desired signature file and click Open.*

Figure 9.79 *The selected signature file now appears in the Identity preferences tab.*

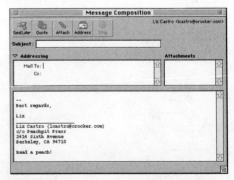

Figure 9.80 *The signature file is automatically copied to each new Message Composition window.*

The Address Book

Figure 10.1 *Choose Address Book in the Window menu.*

Figure 10.2 *The Address Book appears. The addresses it contains are listed in alphabetical order with mailing lists at the end.*

The Address Book window

Netscape lets you save e-mail addresses in the Address Book, a window that you can let float on the screen beside the main Netscape window or hide at your convenience.

The Address Book includes not only the e-mail addresses themselves, but also the recipient's name, a description, and a nickname if desired. The Address Book always lists addresses by their names in alphabetical order.

An address book can also contain *mailing lists* that make it easy to send messages to more than one person at a time. Because a mailing list is actually a collection of *aliases* of addresses and not the addresses themselves, you can include an address in as many mailing lists as desired.

To open the Address Book:

Choose Address Book in the Window menu **(Figure 10.1)**. The Address Book appears **(Figure 10.2)**.

The Address Book window

Adding an address

E-mail addresses tend to be long and hard to remember. You can store e-mail addresses in an address book together with the recipient's name, a description, and a nickname.

To add an address to the Address Book:

1. Open the Address Book window by choosing Address Book in the Window menu.

2. Choose Add User in the Item menu **(Figure 10.3)**. The Address Properties dialog box appears.

3. Enter a short, descriptive, easy-to-remember word for the Nickname **(Figure 10.4)**. You can use the nickname to call up the person's name and e-mail address in a message.

4. Enter the Name of the person or organization that corresponds to the e-mail address. The Name will appear on all correspondence that you send out, and it will identify the incoming and outgoing mail in the Mail window.

5. In the E-mail Address field, type the e-mail address carefully. One mistyped digit or letter can keep your mail from getting to its destination.

6. If desired, enter a description for the address in the Description field.

7. Click OK. The address appears in the Address book in alphabetical order.

✔ Tip

■ The Item menu only appears in the menu bar when the Address Book is active.

Figure 10.3 *Choose Add User in the Item menu.*

Figure 10.4 *The Address Book dialog box appears in which you can enter the desired information.*

Adding an address

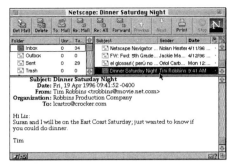

Figure 10.5 *In the Mail or News window, select the message from the person whose address you wish to add to your Address book.*

Figure 10.6 *Choose Add to Address Book in the Message menu.*

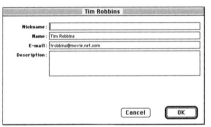

Figure 10.7 *The sender's name and e-mail address are entered in the Address Book dialog box automatically. Enter a nickname and description, if desired, and click OK.*

Figure 10.8 *The new address appears in the Address Book.*

Adding an address from an incoming message

You can add the address of anyone who has sent you a message. Adding an address in this way ensures that the address is not misspelled.

To add an address from incoming messages:

1. Open the message from which you wish to copy the sender's address **(Figure 10.5)**.

2. Choose Add to Address Book in the Message menu **(Figure 10.6)**. The Address Book dialog box appears with the name and address automatically filled in **(Figure 10.7)**.

3. Add a nickname and description if desired. For more information, consult *Adding an address* on page 126.

4. Click OK. The new address is added to your address book **(Figure 10.8)**.

✔ Tips

■ It is possible (and not very hard, as you can see by Figure 10.5) to send mail with a false address. If the sender has not used a real address, you won't be able to use it to write them back irate notes.

■ You can add messages from news postings using this same technique.

Creating a mailing list

The Address Book lets you create a mailing list, similar to the aliases in the Bookmarks window, that lets you send e-mail messages to a whole group of people at the same time.

To create a mailing list:

1. Open the Address Book by choosing Address Book in the Window menu.

2. Choose Add List in the Item menu **(Figure 10.9)**. The New Folder dialog box appears.

3. Enter a short, descriptive, easy-to-remember word for the Nickname **(Figure 10.10)**. You will be able to use the nickname to invoke the list.

4. Type a name for the mailing list in the Name field. A mailing list's name is like a nickname for *all of the addresses* the list contains. As such, it does not appear on any of your correspondence but instead is replaced by the addresses of each person on the list.

5. In the Description field, type a few words that define the list's members.

6. Click OK to save the changes.

7. Select the addresses that you wish to add to the mailing list **(Figure 10.11)**.

8. Drag the names to the new list's icon. Aliases of the addresses are added to the new list while the addresses themselves remain unchanged and in their original positions **(Figure 10.12)**.

✔ Tip

■ You can add more names to the mailing list at any time. Simply drag them on top of the list's icon as in step 8.

Figure 10.9 *Choose Add List in the Item menu.*

Figure 10.10 *In the New Folder dialog box, enter the nickname, name, and description for the mailing list.*

Figure 10.11 *Select the addresses you wish to add to the mailing list. Then drag the selection to the new mailing list.*

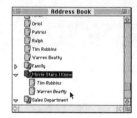

Figure 10.12 *The new mailing list appears in the Address Book with its contents below. Click the triangle at the left of its name to hide (or show) its addresses.*

Creating a mailing list

Figure 10.13 *Double click an address in the Address Book window.*

Figure 10.14 *A pre-addressed Message Composition window appears.*

Using an address or list

The beauty of the Address Book is that you can send e-mail to someone without having to type his address. A list lets you e-mail *several* people at once.

To use an address:

1. Double click the desired address or list in the Address Book **(Fig. 10.13)**.

2. The Message Composition window appears, automatically addressed to the person or list of people selected in step 1 **(Figure 10.14)**.

3. Compose the message as usual.

✔ Tips

- Add an address (or more than one by selecting several first) to an existing mail message by dragging it from the Address Book to the desired field.

- You can tell which field you are dragging an address to by watching the gray line that appears below the field.

- Once in the Message Composition window, click any of the address buttons (Mail to:, Cc:, etc.) to access the Address Book.

- You can also type the nickname in a field in the Message Composition window to add an address to that field. The full address appears when you press Tab to go to the next field.

Changing or deleting an address or list

You may need to change an entry in your address book, for example, if the person changes online services, or to add descriptive information or a nickname.

To change an address or list:

1. Click once on the address or list to select it **(Figure 10.15)** and then choose Edit Address Book Entry in the Item menu **(Figure 10.16)**.

2. In the Address Book dialog box that appears, change the values in the fields as desired **(Figure 10.17)**.

3. Click OK to save the changes.

✔ Tip

■ Hold down the Option key and double click the desired item to edit it.

Getting rid of unused addresses or lists is simple and essential. The cleaner you keep your address book, the easier it will be to find the addresses you *do* use.

To delete an address or list:

1. Select the item you wish to delete in the Address Book by clicking it once.

2. Choose Cut or Delete Address in the Edit menu **(Figure 10.18)**, or hold down the Command key and press Delete. The address or list disappears.

✔ Tip

■ No alert appears when you delete an address, unless the item has an alias. If you delete an address by mistake, choose Undo immediately to bring it back.

Figure 10.15
Select the address or list that you wish to change.

Figure 10.16 *Choose Edit Address Book Entry in the Item menu.*

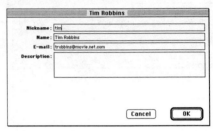

Figure 10.17 *Edit the address or list as desired.*

Figure 10.18 *To delete an address or mailing list, select it and then choose Delete Address (even for a list) in the Edit menu.*

Changing or deleting an address or list

Figure 10.19 *Choose Find in the Edit menu.*

Figure 10.20 *Type the search criteria, select the desired location for the search (although much of this borrowed dialog box pertains to bookmarks) and click Find.*

Figure 10.21 *Netscape highlights the first address that satisfies the criteria. Why is this address highlighted? Check out Figure 10.22.*

Figure 10.22 *The address found in Figure 10.21 contained the search criteria in the Description field.*

Figure 10.23 *To find the next address that satisfies the criteria, choose Find Again in the Edit menu.*

Finding an address

If you have many entries in your address book, it may be hard to find just the address you're looking for. You can search the contents of the Address Book to find the information you need quickly.

To find an address:

1. Choose Find in the Edit menu **(Figure 10.19)**.

2. In the dialog box that appears, type the text that you wish to search for and click Find **(Fig. 10.20)**. Netscape highlights the first entry that satisfies the search criteria **(Figure 10.21)**.

3. If the selected address is not the one you're looking for, choose Find Again in the Edit menu **(Figure 10.23)**. The next entry that satisfies the search criteria is highlighted.

4. Repeat step 3 until you've found the desired address.

✔ Tip

■ Netscape searches in each of the fields in each address. If it's not obvious why a certain address has been highlighted, it's probably because the search criteria was found in one of the fields that is not directly visible from the Address Book window—like Nickname, E-mail Address, or Description **(Figure 10.22)**.

Finding an address

Saving an address book

You can save an address book in order to share it with others or simply to make a back-up copy. In fact, an address book is nothing more than an HTML page that you can browse as you would any other local file.

To save an address book:

1. Choose Save Address Book As in the File menu **(Figure 10.24)**. The Save dialog box appears **(Figure 10.25)**.

2. Give the file a name and choose the folder in which to save it.

3. Click Save to save the file.

✔ Tips

■ If you tack on the extension .html to the end of your address book's name, you'll be able to open the file as a regular Web page *(see page 134)* and share it with other Mac and Unix users. If you give it the .htm extension, you'll be able to read the file with a PC. Each of the addresses in the address book is converted into a link on the Web page.

■ Yes, that is the Save *bookmarks* file dialog box that appears, but it works fine with address books, too.

Figure 10.24 *Choose Save Address Book As in the File menu.*

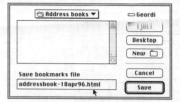

Figure 10.25 *In the Save dialog box, give the address book file a name, preferably with the .html extension. Then click Save.*

Figure 10.26 *Choose Import Addresses in the File menu.*

Figure 10.27 *Select the desired address book file and click Open.*

Figure 10.28 *The new addresses are added to the existing ones in the Address Book window. Addresses with the same names are not replaced, simply added.*

Importing an address book

You can import the addresses from a saved address book file into your current address book. For example, you can save the address book file on your computer at work and then import it into your address book at your home computer.

To import an address book:

1. Choose Import Addresses in the File menu **(Figure 10.26)**. The Import dialog box appears.

2. Choose the address book file that you wish to import and click Open **(Figure 10.27)**. The addresses in the imported file are displayed in the current Address Book window **(Figure 10.28)**.

✔ Tips

■ Currently, Netscape does not replace or update names that already exist. It simply adds the new entries. The only unique part of an address is the nickname. If an incoming address has the same nickname as an existing address, the incoming address' nickname will be lost.

■ To open a different address book file without replacing the existing one, follow the same procedure as described for bookmarks on page 82.

Importing an address book

Opening an address book as a Web page

An easy way to see an address book without changing your regular address book is to open it as a Web page. Since the address book is in HTML format, like any other Web page, Netscape knows how to interpret it correctly, displaying all the addresses as links which can be clicked on to send a message to the corresponding person.

To open an address book as a Web page:

1. Save your address book. *(See "Saving an address book" on page 132.)*

2. Choose Open File in the File menu **(Figure 10.29)**.

3. Choose the desired file and click Open **(Figure 10.30)**. The address book file is loaded into Netscape and each address is automatically converted into a link **(Figure 10.31)**.

✔ Tip

■ You can use this technique to create a Web page that elicits feedback from your readers. Save an address book that contains all of the public relations or technical support people in your company. Then include the address book cum Web page in your site. Your readers will have instant e-mail access to all of the people in the address book.

Figure 10.29 *With a browser active, choose Open File in the File menu.*

Figure 10.30 *In the Open dialog box, choose the desired address book file and click Open.*

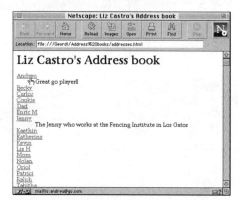

Figure 10.31 *An address book file opened as a Web page appears with each address as a link. Users can click the address to send a message to the corresponding person. (This isn't my real address book file, I confess.)*

The News Window

Figure 11.1 *The upper left pane (enlarged here) lists the news hosts and available newsgroups.*

Figure 11.2 *When you click a newsgroup, its postings are displayed in the upper right pane of the News window (enlarged here).*

Figure 11.3 *A click on a posting reveals the message in the lower pane (enlarged here).*

The News window is Netscape's central command area for displaying the newsgroups available through your server and the postings that belong to each one. From the News window, you can view and subscribe to newsgroups, and read and reply to postings or create your own.

There is an enormous amount of traffic in the newsgroups. The News window lets you flag postings that are important and mark an individual posting, a thread, or even an entire newsgroup as read, so that it doesn't appear the next time you view the newsgroup.

The parts of the News window

The News window is divided into three areas, or panes. The top left panel **(Figure 11.1)** lists the newsgroups, and gives the number of unread and total messages in each, and tells whether you're subscribed. You can choose to view *all* the newsgroups, the *new* newsgroups, only the newsgroups you've *subscribed to,* or only the newsgroups you've subscribed to that *have new messages.*

When you click in one of the newsgroups, a list of the postings it contains appears in the top right pane of the News window **(Figure 11.2)**. Each posting is identified by its Subject, Sender, Date, and whether it has been marked or read.

Once you click a posting, the contents of the message appears in the bottom pane of the News window **(Figure 11.3)**.

The parts of the News window

Using the News window

The most important difference between the News window and the Mail window is that the former shows newsgroups and postings while the latter shows folders and e-mail. Overall, however, their functions are virtually identical:

To get around in the News window, consult *Navigating through your messages* on page 108.

To resize the News window and its individual panes, consult *Changing the size of the panes* on page 102. To resize the columns or change their order, consult *Changing the columns* on page 103.

To choose a font for viewing News messages, consult *Changing your messages' appearance* on page 104.

To sort your postings, consult *Putting your messages in order* on page 98. To view your postings in hierarchical order, instead of strictly by date or sender, consult *Threading messages* on page 101.

To open the News window:

Choose Netscape News in the Window menu **(Figure 11.4)**. The News window is displayed with the news host (if any) listed in the top left pane. (For more information about news hosts, consult *Opening a news host* on page 138.)

To close the News window:

Click the close box in the upper left window of the News window **(Figure 11.5)**.

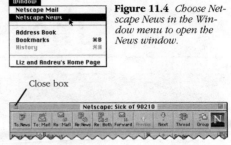

Figure 11.4 *Choose Netscape News in the Window menu to open the News window.*

Figure 11.5 *Click the Close box to close the News window.*

Figure 11.6 *A news host may offer several different categories of newsgroups. Click a triangle to see the individual newsgroups in each section.*

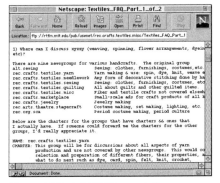

Figure 11.7 *A FAQ (this one is from rec.crafts.textiles) tells what topics are discussed in a particular newsgroup and gives general information about those topics.*

Where newsgroup names come from

There are several major categories of newsgroups: alt (*alternative*, includes a wide variety of groups from alt.sex to alt.appalachian), comp (*computer*, with every program and operating system imaginable), news (*newsgroups*, most contain information about newsgroups themselves), rec (*recreation*, from rec.arts.cinema to rec.games.go to rec.sport.fencing), sci (*science*, from sci.archaeology to sci.virtual-worlds), and soc (*society*, includes the soc.culture newsgroups that discuss different countries and their customs). Your server will probably have access to several more categories, including specialty or local groups **(Figure 11.6)**.

One good way to find out what a newsgroup is about is by reading its FAQ or *frequently asked questions* file, if it has one. Each newsgroup's FAQ is generally posted to the newsgroup once a month. You can find many of them at **ftp://rtfm.mit.edu/pub/usenet/newsgroup.name** where *newsgroup.name* is the full name of the newsgroup in question **(Figure 11.7)**.

Opening a news host

Most people have access to only one news server or host. In general, the news host's name is *news.service-provider-name.com* (or .edu). If you're not sure, contact your Internet service provider. You must open at least one news host so that Netscape knows where to connect to get the data for the newsgroups.

Figure 11.8 *Choose Open News Host in the File menu to set up a new newsgroup server.*

To open a new newsgroup host:

1. With the News window active, choose Open News Host in the File menu **(Figure 11.8)**.

2. In the dialog box that appears, type the name of your news server— something like **news.provider.com**. Consult your Internet provider if you're not sure **(Figure 11.9)**.

3. Click OK. Netscape contacts the news host and, if you have the proper access privileges, shows the news host folder in the left pane of the News window **(Figure 11.10)**.

Figure 11.9 *In the Open News Host dialog box, type the name of the news host (generally* news *followed by the server name).*

Figure 11.10 *The news host appears in the upper left pane of the News window. Sometimes there will already be a few newsgroups showing, but you'll usually still have to download the whole list (see page 139).*

✔ **Tips**

■ Some news hosts restrict access to certain users. Others let anyone connect to see the newsgroups it contains. For example, to see the newsgroups offered to the public by Netscape Communications, open the news host **secnews.netscape.com**. (The name of the Netscape newsgroup is **netscape.navigator**.)

■ You can open as many news hosts as you have access to.

■ To eliminate a news host, select it and choose Remove News Host in the File menu **(Figure 11.11)**. The news host disappears.

Figure 11.11 *To eliminate a news host, choose Remove News Host in the File menu.*

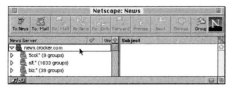

Figure 11.12 *Select the desired news host. Click the triangle to its left to open it.*

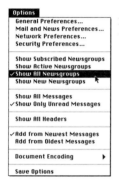

Figure 11.13 *Choose Show All Newsgroups in the Options menu.*

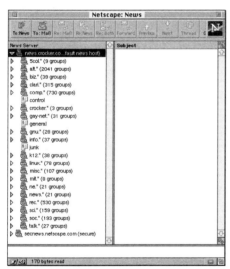

Figure 11.14 *All of the available newsgroups are listed in the left pane. Click a triangle next to a name with an asterisk to see the "subcategories" of newsgroups that it contains.*

Getting a list of all newsgroups

Your Internet service provider decides which newsgroups you have access to and which you don't. Some commercial online services like CompuServe and AOL have gotten a bit of press lately about their efforts to censor certain newsgroups. By downloading the full list from the server, you can see exactly what you get. It also makes it easy to browse through them and subscribe to the ones that interest you *(see page 143).*

To get a list of all newsgroups:

1. Select a news host and then click the triangle next to the news host's name to open it **(Figure 11.12)**.

2. Choose Show All Newsgroups in the Options menu **(Figure 11.13)**. If this is the first time that you've selected this option with this news host, it may take a few minutes. All of the available newsgroups are listed in the upper left pane **(Figure 11.14)**.

✔ Tips

■ Viewing all the newsgroups is useful for finding new newsgroups. You can then create a subset of newsgroups that interest you and hide the rest. For more information on choosing a subset, consult *Subscribing to a newsgroup* on page 143. For more details on hiding the newsgroups that don't interest you, consult *Showing only subscribed newsgroups* on page 144.

■ Click the triangle next to a name with an asterisk to see all the newsgroups in that category. Click it again to hide them.

Getting a list of new newsgroups

New newsgroups are added all the time. All it takes is a group of people who write a charter, elicit votes from the potential public, and then distribute the new newsgroups to the Internet. You can display the newsgroups which have been added since the last time you checked.

To get a list of new newsgroups:

1. Select the desired news host and click the triangle to its left **(Figure 11.15)**.

2. With the News window active, choose Show New Newsgroups in the Options menu **(Figure 11.16)**. A message will appear that tells you how many new newsgroups have been added, if any, since the last time you used this command **(Figure 11.17 and Figure 11.18)**.

3. Click OK. The new newsgroups are displayed at the end of the current newsgroup list **(Figure 11.19)**.

✔ Tip

■ You are not automatically subscribed to new newsgroups. For more information on subscribing, consult *Subscribing to a newsgroup* on page 143.

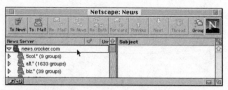

Figure 11.15 *Select a news host and click the triangle to its left to open it.*

Figure 11.16 *Choose Show New Newsgroups in the Options menu.*

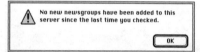

Figure 11.17 *Netscape will show an alert if no newgroups have been created since the last time you used this command.*

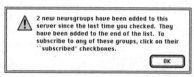

Figure 11.18 *If new newsgroups have been created since the last time you checked, Netscape will tell you how many there are and that they will be listed at the bottom of the current list.*

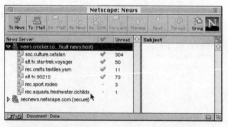

Figure 11.19 *Netscape lists the new newsgroup(s)—rec.sport.rodeo and rec.aquaria.freshwater.cichlids, in this example—at the end of your current list.*

Figure 11.20 *With the News window active, choose Add Newsgroup in the File menu.*

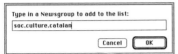

Figure 11.21 *In the dialog box that appears, type the full name of the newsgroup that you want to subscribe to.*

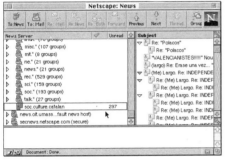

Figure 11.22 *The new newsgroup appears at the end of the list in the left pane. You are not automatically subscribed to it.*

Viewing a newsgroup by name

If you know the name of a newsgroup, you don't have to sort through the full list in order to view it.

To view a newsgroup when you know its name:

1. With the News window active, choose Add Newsgroup in the File menu **(Figure 11.20)**.

2. In the dialog box that appears, type the full name of the newsgroup that you want to view **(Figure 11.21)**.

3. Click OK. The newsgroup appears in the left pane of the News window **(Figure 11.22)**.

✔ Tip

■ You are not automatically subscribed to a newsgroup when you view it. For more information, consult *Subscribing to a newsgroup* on page 143.

Viewing a newsgroup by name

Viewing a newsgroup from other windows

You can view, and then subscribe to, a newsgroup from the browser or the Mail window. If you know the newsgroup's name, you can type it in the Location field in the browser. In addition, if you encounter a link to the newsgroup, either on a Web page or in an e-mail message, you can click the link to view the newsgroup.

To use the Location field in the browser to view a newsgroup:

1. In the main Netscape window, type **news:newsgroup.address** in the Location field, where *newsgroup.address* is the complete name of the newsgroup that you wish to view **(Figure 11.23)**. Netscape automatically displays the News window with the selected newsgroup at the bottom of the list in the left pane **(Figure 11.24)**.

2. Click the newsgroup's name to display the messages in the right pane of the News window.

To jump to a newsgroup from a Web page or e-mail:

1. Click the link on the Web page or e-mail message **(Fig. 11.25)**. The News window opens and displays the newsgroup in the left pane **(Fig. 11.26)**.

2. Click the newsgroup's name to view its messages in the right pane.

✔ Tip

■ You are not automatically subscribed to a newsgroup when you view it *(see page 143)*.

Figure 11.23 *Type* **news:** *followed by the newsgroup's name in the Location field in the main Netscape window. (When you start to type, Location changes to Go to:.)*

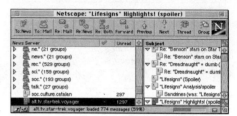

Figure 11.24 *The newsgroup appears at the bottom of the list and its messages appear in the right pane.*

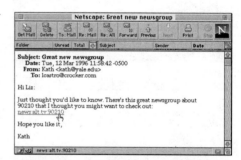

Figure 11.25 *Click a link to a newsgroup from a Web page or an e-mail message.*

Figure 11.26 *Netscape automatically switches to the News window and shows the newsgroup at the bottom of the list and its messages in the right pane.*

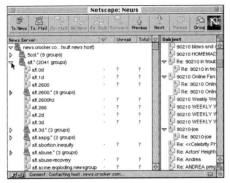

Figure 11.27 *Scroll around in the list of newsgroups in the left pane until you see the one that you want to subscribe to. You can click the triangles next to a folder to open it (or click the triangle again to close a folder).*

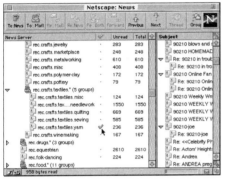

Figure 11.28 *Click the box next to the newsgroup's name to subscribe to it. A blue checkmark will appear.*

Subscribing to a newsgroup

You can browse through the postings in any newsgroup from the full list *(see page 139)*. However, since there are over 14,000 individual newsgroups, it is handy to select a few that you wish to follow and hide the rest. Selecting a newsgroup is called *subscribing* to it.

To subscribe to a newsgroup:

1. Use the techniques described on the preceding pages to show the desired newsgroup in the upper left pane of the News window **(Figure 11.27)**.

2. Click in the Subscribed column (the one headed by ☑), directly to the right of the newsgroup's name **(Figure 11.28)**. A blue checkmark appears next to the newsgroup to show that you have subscribed to it.

To cancel a subscription to a newsgroup:

Click the blue checkmark next to a newsgroup's name to cancel a subscription. The blue checkmark disappears.

✔ Tip

■ You can subscribe to as many newsgroups as you like. The idea, of course, is to subscribe to the ones that you will actually read, and then hide the rest. You can always go back to the main list.

Showing only subscribed newsgroups

Once you have subscribed to each newsgroup in which you are interested, you can hide the rest. You can also choose to view only the newsgroups to which you are subscribed that have new messages (since the last time you checked).

To show only the newsgroups that you have subscribed to:

1. Select a news host in the News window.

2. Choose Show Subscribed Newsgroups in the Options menu **(Figure 11.29)**. The extra newsgroups are hidden and only the newsgroups that you have subscribed to are shown **(Fig. 11.30)**.

Some of the newsgroups to which you have subscribed may have many new messages added each day. Others may not see any action during weeks. You can choose to display only those newsgroups to which you have subscribed that have *new* messages.

To show only the newsgroups with new messages:

1. Select a news host in the News window.

2. Choose Show Active Newsgroups in the Options menu **(Figure 11.31)**. Only the newsgroups to which you are subscribed that have new messages are displayed **(Figure 11.32)**.

Figure 11.29 *With the News window active, choose Show Subscribed Newsgroups in the Options menu.*

Figure 11.30 *Only the newsgroups that you have subscribed to (marked by a blue check-mark) are shown in the left pane of the News window.*

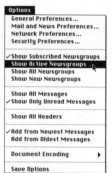

Figure 11.31 *With the News window active, choose Show Active Newsgroups in the Options menu.*

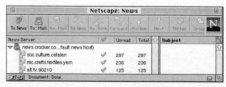

Figure 11.32 *Netscape only shows those newsgroups that have messages that you haven't read yet. (Notice that the alt.tv.star-trek.voyager newsgroup that appeared in Figure 11.30 does not appear here, because it has no unread messages.)*

144

Figure 11.33 *A green diamond appears next to the new, unread messages.*

Figure 11.34 *After selecting the desired message, choose Mark as Read in the Message menu.*

Figure 11.35 *The message marked as read loses its diamond.*

Figure 11.36 *After selecting any one message in the thread, choose Mark Thread Read in the Message menu (left) or click the Mark Thread button in the toolbar (right).*

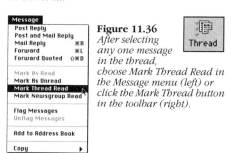

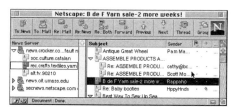

Figure 11.37 *All the messages in the thread are marked as read: the green diamonds disappear.*

Marking messages as read

Some newsgroups get an awful lot of traffic. If you don't have enough time to read every message, you can mark them as read so that they don't appear the next time you open that newsgroup.

To mark messages as read:

1. Select the messages that you wish to mark as read **(Figure 11.33)**.

2. Choose Mark as Read or Mark as Unread in the Message menu **(Figure 11.34)**. Read messages no longer carry a green diamond **(Figure 11.35)**.

To mark a thread as read:

1. Select a message in the thread. You don't need to select all of them.

2. Choose Mark Thread as Read in the Message menu **(Figure 11.36)**. The messages in the thread no longer display a green diamond **(Figure 11.37)**.

✔ Tips

- You can hide read messages. For more information, consult *Hiding read messages* on page 147.

- You can also click the Mark Thread button on the toolbar to mark a thread as read **(Figure 11.36)**. Click the green diamond next to any message to mark it as read. Click it again to mark it as unread.

- For more information about threaded messages, consult *Threading messages* on page 101.

Marking an entire newsgroup as read

Sometimes you'll want to mark an entire newsgroup as read so that the next time you open the newsgroup you'll be sure that the messages are new.

To mark an entire newsgroup as read:

1. Select the newsgroup—or any message in the newsgroup—that you wish to mark as read **(Figure 11.38)**.

2. Choose Mark Newsgroup Read in the Message menu **(Figure 11.39)**. All the messages in the newsgroup are marked as read **(Figure 11.40)**.

✔ Tip

■ You can also click the Mark Group button on the toolbar to mark a group as read **(Figure 11.41)**.

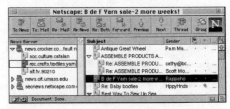

Figure 11.38 *Choose a newsgroup that you wish to mark as read. (You can also mark a message within the newsgroup.)*

Figure 11.39 *Select Mark Newsgroup Read in the Message menu.*

Figure 11.40 *All the messages in the newsgroup are marked as read; the green diamonds disappear.*

Figure 11.41 *You can also click the Mark Group button to mark a newsgroup as read.*

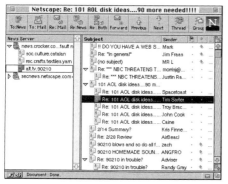

Figure 11.42 *When you read a message or mark it as read, the green diamond no longer appears next to it.*

Figure 11.43 *Choose Show Only Unread Messages in the Options menu.*

Figure 11.44 *Only the unread messages are shown.*

Hiding read messages

Once you've read a message, you can make it disappear so that it's easier to find the messages you *haven't* read yet.

To hide read messages:

Choose Show Only Unread Messages in the Options menu **(Figure 11.43)**. The messages that you've read—or marked as read—disappear **(Figure 11.44)**.

To show both read and unread messages:

Choose Show All Messages in the Options menu. Both the messages that you've read as well as those you haven't appear in the right pane.

✔ Tip

■ If you had already selected Show Only Unread Messages in the Options menu, and then read a few messages, the messages don't disappear as you read them. In fact, selecting the option again has no effect. First, you have to select Show All Messages and *then* choose Show Only Unread Messages. Seems like a bug to me.

Hiding read messages

Getting more messages

Although some newsgroups can contain hundreds or even thousands of messages at a time, Netscape will only load a certain number of these to start. For example, the newsgroup may contain 1,238 messages but Newsgroup will load only 100 at a time. Once you're through with the first one hundred, you can load in more.

To get more messages:

1. Select the desired newsgroup (or any message that it contains) **(Fig. 11.45)**.

2. Choose Get More Messages in the File menu or click the Get More Messages icon in the bottom right corner of the window **(Figure 11.46)**. Netscape displays the new set of messages.

To change the number of messages loaded at a time:

1. Choose Mail and News Preferences in the Options menu. The Preferences box appears. Click the Server tab **(Figure 11.47)**.

2. Type a new number in the text box next to Get xx Messages at a time.

3. Click OK to close the dialog box.

✔ Tip

■ In the Options menu, choose Add from Newest Messages if you want to load in messages starting with the most recently posted ones. Choose Add from Oldest Messages if you want to load in messages starting from the oldest ones.

Figure 11.45 *Select the desired newsgroup by clicking it (or by selecting one of its postings).*

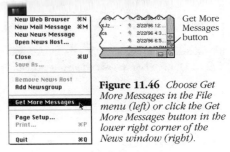

Figure 11.46 *Choose Get More Messages in the File menu (left) or click the Get More Messages button in the lower right corner of the News window (right).*

Figure 11.47 *Type in the number of messages that you wish to load at one time in the News section at the bottom of the Servers preferences tab.*

Getting more messages

Reading and Posting News

Figure 12.1 *Click the newsgroup's name in the left pane of the News window.*

Figure 12.2 *Click a message in the right pane to display its contents in the lower pane.*

Figure 12.3 *When you're reading messages, make the right pane wider so that you can see the title of each message more clearly.*

The main difference between working with newsgroups and using e-mail is that newsgroup postings disappear, while mail remains on your hard disk.

Reading the postings in a newsgroup

You don't have to subscribe to a newsgroup *(see page 143)* in order to read the postings that it contains.

To read a newsgroup's postings:

1. Click the newsgroup in the left pane of the News window **(Fig. 12.1)**. The postings are shown in the right pane of the News window.

2. Click a posting in the right pane to display its contents in the lower pane of the News window **(Figure 12.2)**.

3. Use the scroll bars to view more of the message as necessary.

4. Navigate to read more messages *(see page 108)*.

✔ Tips

■ Adjust the width of the panes to suit the task at hand **(Figure 12.3)**. For more information, see *Changing the size of the panes* on page 102.

■ You can show additional information about a message, including the route it took to get to you (which is sometimes useful for exposing fraudulent messages), by choosing Show All Headers in the Options menu.

Posting a message to a newsgroup

With e-mail, you can only send messages to people you already know, or at least have the address of. In a newsgroup, you can post a message that may be seen by thousands of people you've never met. The fine distinction about posting messages to a newsgroup is the topic. You should restrict your subject matter to that which is usually discussed in that newsgroup. Check the FAQ if you're not sure *(see page 137)*.

To post a message to a newsgroup:

1. In the News window, select the newsgroup—or a message in that group—where you want to post a message **(Figure 12.4)**.

2. Choose New News Message in the File menu or click the To: News button **(Figure 12.5)**. A fresh Message Composition window appears. The selected newsgroup is automatically filled in in the Newsgroups field **(Figure 12.6)**.

3. Type the subject of the message in the Subject field **(Figure 12.7)**. The subject is important: as the most visible part of the message, it can mean the difference between people reading your message or ignoring it.

4. Type the contents of the message in the area at the bottom of the window.

5. Choose Send Mail Now (or Send Mail Later) in the File menu or click the Send button to send the message **(Figure 12.8)**.

Figure 12.4 *In the News window, select the newsgroup—or a posting in that group—to which you wish to post a message.*

Figure 12.5 *Choose New News Message in the File menu (left) or click the To: News button on the toolbar (right).*

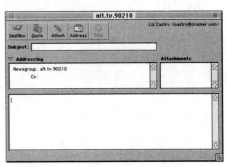

Figure 12.6 *The Message Composition window appears with the name of the newsgroup automatically entered in the Newsgroups field.*

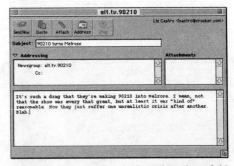

Figure 12.7 *Type the subject in the Subject field and the contents of the posting in the lower area.*

Figure 12.8
Choose Send Mail Now (or Later) in the File menu or click the Send button on the toolbar.

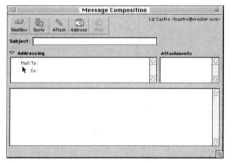

Figure 12.9 *If the Newsgroups field does not appear, you probably didn't choose a newsgroup before selecting New News Message.*

Figure 12.10 *Simply choose Newsgroups in the View menu to make the Newsgroups field appear in the Message Composition window.*

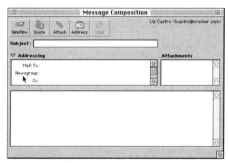

Figure 12.11 *The Newsgroups field appears. Now you can type the name of the newsgroup and post the message.*

✔ **Tips**

■ Posting a message is virtually the same as sending e-mail. The only difference is that an e-mail message requires use of the Mail To field, while a news posting uses the Newsgroups field.

■ Click the Address button to make the Address Book appear.

■ By default, your messages are posted immediately—although it may take a little while before they appear in the newsgroup. For information on deferred posting, consult *Composing postings offline* on page 153.

■ If the Newsgroups field doesn't appear, you probably didn't select the newsgroup before opening the Message Composition window **(Figure 12.9)**. Choose Newsgroups in the View menu **(Figure 12.10)** to make the field appear **(Figure 12.11)** and type in the newsgroup's name. For more information on message parts, consult *Viewing or hiding the parts of a message* on page 110.

■ You can post a message to several newsgroups at once. Separate each additional newsgroup name with a comma.

■ You attach a URL or file to a news message in exactly the same way as you attach one to an e-mail message. For more information, consult *Attaching files to a message* on page 120 or *Attaching a URL to a message* on page 121.

Posting a message to a newsgroup

Replying to a newsgroup post

There are three ways to respond to a message in a newsgroup. If you want everyone in the newsgroup to see your reply, post the response to the newsgroup. If you only want the original sender to receive the reply, e-mail him or her directly. Finally, you can simultaneously post and mail a message to cover all your bases.

To reply to a newsgroup post:

1. Select the message that you wish to reply to in the upper right pane of the News window **(Figure 12.12)**.

2. In the Message menu, choose Post Reply to have your reply appear in the newsgroup **(Fig. 12.13)**. Choose Mail Reply to e-mail your reply only to the writer of the original message **(Fig. 12.14)**. Choose Post and Send Reply to do both things **(Fig. 12.15)**.

3. The Message Composition window appears, with the appropriate fields automatically filled in. The Newsgroups field only appears in postings, the Mail To field only appears in mail.

4. Choose Send Now (or Send Later) in the File menu.

✔ Tips

■ Generally, you are supposed to try and limit your postings to information that will interest the entire newsgroup. Mail a response when it applies only to the particular recipient.

■ Sometimes, people post messages and then don't check to see if they have any responses. You can post and mail a message to make sure that both the newsgroup members and the recipient receive (and see) a copy.

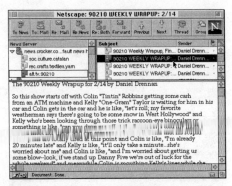

Figure 12.12 *Select the posting that you want to reply to in the right pane of the News window.*

Figure 12.13 *Choose Post Reply in the Message menu (left) to publish the posting in the newsgroup. Notice that the Newsgroup field appears but that the Mail To field does not (right).*

Figure 12.14 *Choose Mail Reply in the Message menu (left) to mail the posting to the original sender. Notice that the Mail To field appears but the Newsgroups field does not (right).*

Figure 12.15 *Choose Post and Mail Reply in the Message menu (left) to publish the posting in the newsgroup and send a copy to the original sender. Notice that both the Newsgroups and Mail To fields appear (right).*

Figure 12.16
Choose New News Message in the File menu (left) or click the To: News button in the toolbar (right).

Figure 12.17 *Type the message in the Message Composition window.*

Figure 12.18 *Choose Deferred Delivery in the Options menu.*

Figure 12.19 *Choose Send Mail Later in the File menu (left) or click the Send Later button (right) on the toolbar.*

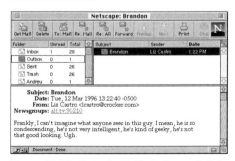

Figure 12.20 *Go to the Mail window and click the Outbox to see the outbound posting.*

Composing postings offline

When you receive an e-mail message, Netscape downloads it to your hard disk, making it easy to reply to later, even if you're not connected to your Internet account. However, when you read a news posting, the message is not downloaded to your hard disk. So even though you can compose a new posting or a reply offline, you can't browse the existing messages and respond to them directly.

To compose postings offline:

1. Disconnect from the Internet without quitting Netscape (or launch Netscape without connecting to the Internet).

2. Choose New News Message in the File menu **(Figure 12.16)**. The Message Composition window appears.

3. Compose the posting as usual *(see pages 150 and 152)* **(Figure 12.17)**. If you are replying to a posting, type **Re: subject** in the Subject field where *subject* is the original topic.

4. In the Message Composition window's Options menu, choose Deferred Delivery **(Figure 12.18)**.

5. Choose Send Mail Later in the File menu or click the Send button on the toolbar **(Figure 12.19)**. The message is stored in the Outbox **(Figure 12.20)** in the Mail window .

6. When you're ready to send the posting(s), consult *Sending the messages in the Outbox* on page 113.

✔ Tip

■ Leave the newsgroup open before disconnecting and make the window as large as possible, so that you can at least see all the postings' subject lines.

Composing postings offline

153

Sending mail from the News window

Figure 12.21 *With the News window active, choose New Mail Message in the File menu.*

Reading a posting in the News window may motivate you to write someone. Perhaps it will just spark your imagination, perhaps you'll want to tell her about something you've read or offer a link to a newsgroup. At any rate, the process is virtually identical to sending e-mail from the Mail window.

To send mail from the News window:

1. Choose New Mail Message in the File menu or click To: Mail on the toolbar **(Fig. 12.21)**. The Message Composition window appears **(Figure 12.22)**.

2. Compose the message as usual *(see page 109)*.

3. If desired, add a link to the newsgroup that inspired you by typing **news:name.newsgroup** in the message area where *name.newsgroup* is the complete name of the newsgroup **(Figure 12.23)**. If the recipient reads the message with Netscape 2, the newsgroup will appear as a link, and a click on it will open the newsgroup for him or her **(Figure 12.24)**.

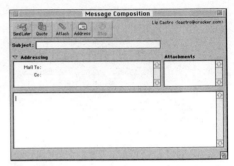

Figure 12.22 *An empty Message Composition window appears.*

Figure 12.23 *Compose your message as usual. If you want to add a link to a newsgroup, type its name preceded by **news:**.*

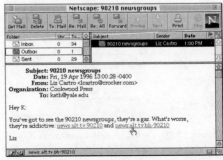

Figure 12.24 *The newsgroups appear as links in the message, once it is sent.*

Part III:
Preferences

155

General Preferences

Figure 13.1 *Choose General Preferences in the Options menu.*

The settings in the General Preferences dialog box control many different aspects of Netscape. To access the General Preferences box, choose General Preferences in the Options menu **(Figure 13.1)**.

The General Preferences dialog box is divided into seven sections called *tabs*. Click a tab's name to make it active and access its settings. Each tab is described in detail in the following pages.

Once you've made the desired changes to the settings, click OK to save the changes, or Cancel to leave the dialog box without saving them. Click Help to access Netscape's Help file.

General Preferences

Appearance

Click the Appearance tab in the General
Preferences dialog box to display the
Appearance preferences. Use the
Appearance preferences to control the
appearance of the toolbar, the initial
window (and page) that Netscape
shows upon launch, and links.

Toolbars —
Startup —
Link Styles —

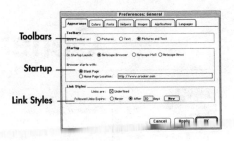

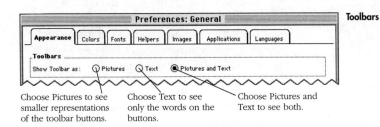

Toolbars

Choose Pictures to see
smaller representations
of the toolbar buttons.

Choose Text to see
only the words on the
buttons.

Choose Pictures and
Text to see both.

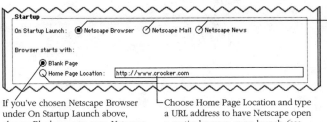

Startup

Click Netscape Browser so that
the first window you see when
entering Netscape is the Web
Browser. Click Netscape Mail to
start with the Mail window (and
automatically check your mail).
Click Netscape News to start
with the News window.

If you've chosen Netscape Browser
under On Startup Launch above,
choose Blank page to open Netscape
with a clean, blank window *(see
page 14)*.

Choose Home Page Location and type
a URL address to have Netscape open
a particular page upon launch *(see
page 14)*.

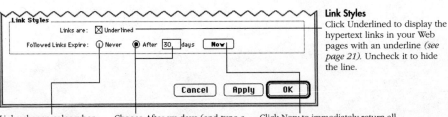

Link Styles

Click Underlined to display the
hypertext links in your Web
pages with an underline *(see
page 21)*. Uncheck it to hide
the line.

Links change color when
you click them. Choose
Never to keep the "visited"
color forever.

Choose After xx days (and type a
number of days) to have the links
return to their original color after
a certain number of days.

Click Now to immediately return all
links to their unclicked color.

Appearance

Colors

You have some control over the colors used on the pages you browse. You can choose a different color for new and visited links and for regular text. For the background, choose either a color or an image. Finally, you can make these choices override the options used in any individual Web page.

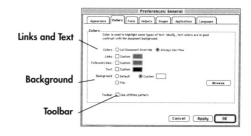

Links and Text

Background

Toolbar

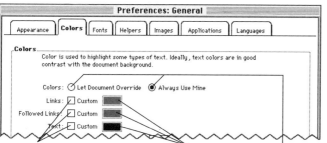

To change a color, first click the Custom button.

The current color is shown in the swatch. After clicking Custom, click the color swatch and then choose a new color in the dialog box that appears.

Links and Text
You can choose your own colors for links you haven't visited (Links), links you have visited (Followed Links) and for regular text (Text). Simply click Custom and then click Choose Color. Choose a color in the dialog box that appears and click OK. The new color will be shown in the swatch.

To view the colors as designed for a Web page, choose Let Document Override. To always use the colors defined in this dialog box, choose Always Use Mine.

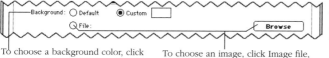

To choose a background color, click Custom and then click the color swatch. Choose a color for the background in the dialog box that appears.

To choose an image, click Image file, then click Browse and locate the desired file (GIF or JPEG format) on your hard disk.

Background
You may choose a special color or even an image for the background of all the pages you browse.

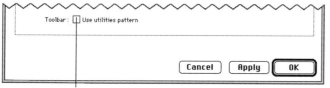

Toolbar
You can choose your own pattern for the toolbar.

Click Use utilities pattern to change the background pattern of the toolbar. You set the utilities pattern by opening the Desktop Patterns control panel, choosing a pattern, holding down the Option key and clicking Set Utilities Pattern.

Colors

Fonts

Click the Fonts tab in the General Preferences dialog box to display the Fonts preferences. Use the Fonts preferences to choose the default font encoding for the documents you browse, as well as the particular fonts that should be used.

Encoding

Choose Fonts

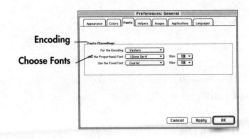

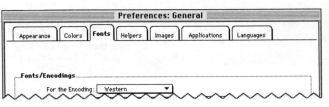

Encoding
Choose an encoding that matches the alphabet of the documents you will read. An encoding describes the relationship between characters and their hexadecimal representations.

Most of the text you see in a document will be displayed with a proportional font like Times or Helvetica.

The text displayed in entry forms and sometimes in block quotes or other special parts of a page is displayed with a fixed font like Courier.

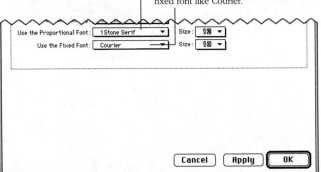

Choose Fonts
Select a font and size in each pop-up menu.

Helpers

Click the Helpers tab in the General Preferences dialog box to see the Helpers preferences. You can choose which helper applications should be launched according to which files Netscape encounters out on the Web, or if the files should simply be saved.

List of file types

File type

Action

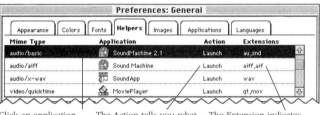

List of File Types
Many different kinds of files are listed, along with the action that will take place when Netscape encounters them, and the extensions that define those kinds of files.

Click an application type to change its options.

The Action tells you what Netscape will do when it encounters this type of file.

The Extension indicates what kinds of files are included in the File type.

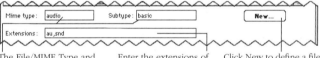

File Type
This section defines the file type, lets you choose a new file type, and lets you see (or add) new extensions.

The File/MIME Type and Subtype give the same information as in the scroll list above, for the selected type.

Enter the extensions of the files that you wish to define as the selected File type.

Click New to define a file type for a kind of file not already in the list.

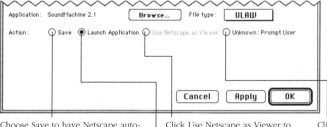

Action
You tell Netscape what you want to do with each kind of file it finds. You can view the file directly (if Netscape can), save it, have it ask you, or launch a helper application that, in turn, opens the file.

Choose Save to have Netscape automatically save the files with this extension to your hard disk.

Click Use Netscape as Viewer to view the file in Netscape, if possible.

Click Unknown: Prompt User to have Netscape ask you what to do when it encounters a file type that it doesn't recognize.

Choose Launch Application (and click Browse and find the application on your hard disk) to have Netscape automatically open a program that can open the files that have this extension.

Images

Click the Images tab in the General Preferences dialog box to display the Images preferences. You can choose the method in which extra colors should be displayed and how images should be loaded onto the page.

Display Images

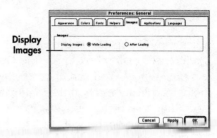

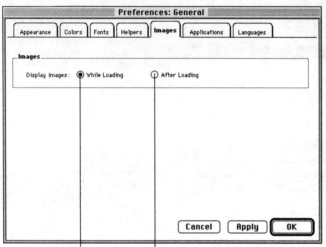

Choose While Loading if you want to see the images as they load.

Choose After Loading to display the images all at once, after all the data has been received. On a fast network, this may be slightly faster.

Display Images

If you have chosen Auto Load Images in the Options menu, Netscape will load images as it loads each page. With the preferences in this section, you can choose to display the images incrementally while loading, or display them all at once, when all the information has been received.

Applications

Click the Applications tab in the General Preferences dialog box to see the application preferences for the programs you use in conjunction with Netscape. You can also choose the program that you wish to use to view HTML tags *(see page 208)* and the folder where temporary files should be stored.

Telnet Applications

View Source

Temporary Directory

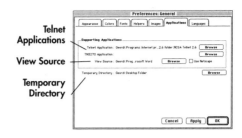

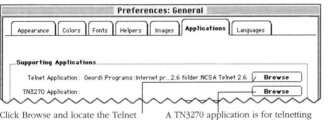

Click Browse and locate the Telnet application that you wish to use. Telnetting means connecting to a remote computer as if you were there in person.

A TN3270 application is for telnetting to an IBM mainframe. Click Browse to locate the desired TN3270 application on your hard disk.

Telnet Applications
You can designate a Telnet or TN3270 application of your choice for connecting to another computer via Telnet through Netscape.

Click Browse to locate the desired program with which to view a page's HTML tags, when you select Document Source in the View menu. For example, you might choose to view HTML tags with Microsoft Word or Word Perfect.

Click Use Netscape to view HTML tags in Netscape's built-in viewer.

View Source
You can choose which program to launch when viewing HTML tags.

Click Browse and choose the folder in which temporary files should be kept.

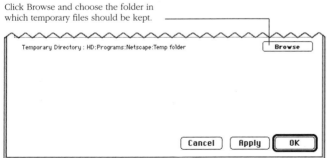

Temporary Directory
When Netscape encounters a file it cannot display by itself, it downloads the file and launches a helper application to deal with it. Once the file has been viewed, it is deleted. You can choose where these temporary files should be kept on your hard disk.

Applications

Language

Click the Language tab in the General Preferences dialog box to see the language preferences. When a page on the Web is available in more than one language, you can tell the server what language(s) you prefer to browse by creating an "accept list" of languages.

Accept Language

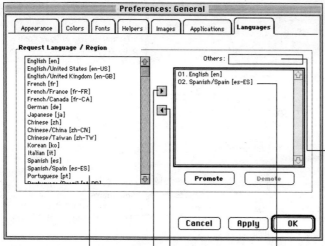

Accept Language
You can create a priority list of languages in which you prefer files to be downloaded or viewed through the Accept list. Then Netscape advises the server of the desired languages and if the server understands, it gives you access to the appropriate language version.

If the desired language or region does not appear in the left list, enter the non-standard language or region and then click the down arrow to add it to the accept list. The first tag should be a two letter ISSO 639 language abbreviation. The second two letters should be an ISO 3166 country tag.

Click a Language/Region in the left list to select it.

Click the right pointing arrow to add the new language to the accept list. Click the left pointing arrow to remove a language from the Accept list.

The acceptable languages are listed in the right list in order of preference.

Mail and News Prefs

Figure 14.1 *Choose Mail and News Preferences in the Options menu to view the Mail and News Preferences dialog box.*

The settings in the Mail and News Preferences dialog box control many different aspects of the mail and news windows. To access the Mail and News Preferences dialog box, choose Mail and News Preferences in the Options menu **(Figure 14.1)**.

The Mail and News Preferences dialog box is divided into five sections called *tabs*. Click a tab's name to make it active and access its settings. Each tab is described in detail in the following pages.

Once you've made the desired changes to the settings, click OK to save the changes, or Cancel to leave the dialog box without saving them. Click Help to access Netscape's Help file.

Mail and News Preferences

Appearance

Click the Appearance tab in the Mail and
News Preferences dialog box to change
the way messages appear in the Mail
and News windows. You can choose the
font that messages should be displayed
in, as well as the style and size of quoted
sections.

Message Font

Styles for
Quoted Text

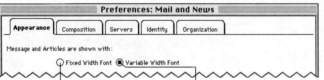

Click Fixed Width Font to use the font
defined next to "Use the Fixed Font"
in the Fonts section of the General
Preferences dialog box.

Click Variable Width Font to use the
font defined next to "Use the Proportional Font" in the Fonts section of the
General Preferences dialog box.

Message Font
In the General Preferences box
(see page 158), you chose a specific font for proportional text and
another for fixed font text. Here,
you can choose which of those
fonts should be used for displaying messages in the Mail and
News windows. (Unfortunately,
the Message Composition window
is not affected.)

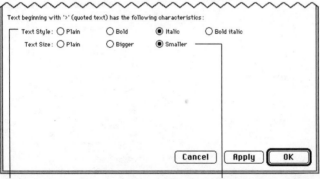

Click Plain, Bold, Italic or Bold Italic
to format quoted text with the corresponding style.

Click Plain to keep the quoted text at
the same size as regular text. Choose
Bigger or Smaller to change the size of
quoted text.

Styles for Quoted Text
Many messages contain text from
earlier correspondence. You can
format that text with a special style
and size to set it apart from the
current message's contents.

Composition

Click the Composition tab in the Mail and News Preferences dialog box to choose a bit format for your messages, whether or not to e-mail or save a copy of them, and if Netscape should automatically quote the original message when you compose its reply.

Format

Saving Outgoing Messages

Automatic Quoting

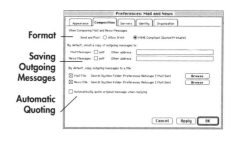

Format

Most e-mail servers in the US and Europe use 8 bit messages. If you are receiving messages from a MIME mail reader, you can change the setting to see the characters correctly.

Click Allow 8-bit for widest compatibility with e-mail servers in the US and Europe.

Click MIME Compliant to make Netscape interpret messages from MIME mail readers correctly.

Saving Outgoing Messages

Incoming mail messages are automatically saved to your hard disk. Outgoing e-mail and news messages are not. Use these options to save these messages automatically.

Type an e-mail address in Mail Messages or News Messages to send a copy of all outgoing messages to that address. Check the self box to send copies to your own e-mail address as entered in the Identity tab *(see page 169)*.

Enter a path on your hard disk in Mail File or News File by clicking Browse in order to save a copy of all outgoing messages to your hard disk.

Automatic Quoting

When you reply to an e-mail message or news posting, it's often a good idea to remind the recipient what they were talking about by quoting their original message. You can have Netscape quote messages all the time (using this option) or just sometimes *(see page 116)*.

Mark the Automatically quote original message when replying checkbox to have Netscape automatically quote the original message in the Message Composition window when you select Reply or Reply to All in the Message menu.

Composition

Servers

Click the Servers tab in the Mail and
News Preferences dialog box to enter
information about the server name, your
name, where mail should be stored,
how large messages can be, whether
they should be left on the server, and if
Netscape should check for mail automatically.

Mail Server
Data

Mail:
Miscellaneous

News:
Miscellaneous

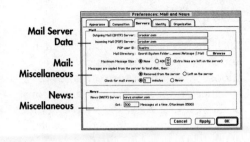

Servers

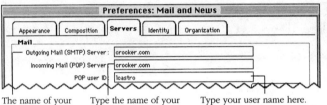

The name of your
Outgoing Mail
Server goes here.

Type the name of your
Incoming Mail Server
here.

Type your user name here.
This is the part of your e-mail
address before the @ symbol.

Mail Server Data
You won't be able to send or
receive mail until you fill in this
important data. If you are not sure
what to put in, ask your service
provider.

Enter the path to the
directory on your hard
disk where mail mes-
sages should be stored
by clicking the Browse
button.

You can limit Mail mes-
sages to a certain size by
choosing a Size. Other-
wise, click None.

Have Netscape check for
mail automatically by clicking Every and entering a
number of minutes. Other-
wise, click Never.

Netscape automatically copies
incoming mail to your hard
disk. Choose whether to leave
a copy on the server as well.

Mail: Miscellaneous
Choose where to store mail messages on your hard disk, their
maximum size, whether or not to
remove them from the server, and
if Netscape should check for mail
automatically.

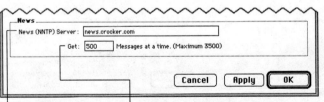

Enter the name of your
news server here. Ask
your service provider if
you're not sure.

Choose how many news messages should
be loaded from a newsgroup at once. The
default is 100.

News: Miscellaneous
In this area, you enter the name of
your news server (ask your Service
Provider), and choose how many
messages you want to retrieve at
a time.

Identity

Click the Identity tab in the Mail and News Preferences box to enter information about yourself, including your name, e-mail address, the e-mail address where you want to receive replies, and the name of your organization. You can also specify a signature file that will be appended to every outgoing message.

Personal Information

Signature File

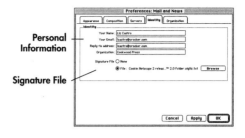

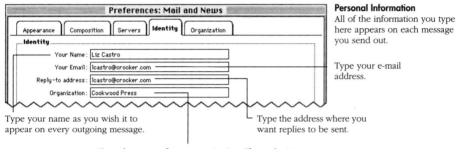

Type your name as you wish it to appear on every outgoing message.

Type the address where you want replies to be sent.

Type the name of your organization. If you don't type anything here, Netscape will use the name of your service provider automatically in all outgoing correspondence.

Personal Information
All of the information you type here appears on each message you send out.

Type your e-mail address.

Click Browse to locate your signature file (any text file) on the hard disk. For more information on signatures, consult *Creating a signature file* on page 123.

Signature File
You can create a text file and then have Netscape automatically add it the end of each message you send. Most signatures include the writer's name, e-mail address, sometimes their snail-mail address, and a cute quote. The only requirement is that it be saved in Text Only format.

Identity

Organization

Click the Organization tab in the Mail
and News preferences dialog box to set
certain defaults for the Mail and News
windows. You can have Netscape
remember your password, and automatically thread and sort messages as
desired

General

Sort

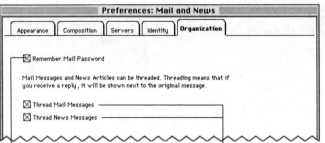

General
You'll need to let Netscape
remember your password if you
want it to check your mail automatically every few minutes.
Threading your messages shows
replies under the original message,
slightly indented.

Click Remember Mail Password so that Netscape doesn't ask you to enter the password
each time you check your mail. You must
check this box if you want Netscape to check
your mail automatically.

You can choose to thread mail or news
messages by default. For more information, consult *Threading messages* on
page 101.

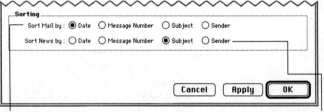

Sort
You can choose default settings
for the order in which Netscape
sorts both Mail and News
messages. For more information
on sorting mail and news messages, consult *Putting your messages in order* on page 98.

Click Date to order mail messages by date, Subject
to order them by subject, and yes, Sender to order
them by Sender, by default, each time you open
the Mail window.

Click Date to order news postings by date, Subject
to order them by subject, and Sender to order them
by Sender, by default, each time you open the
News window.

Network Preferences

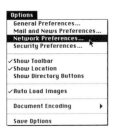

Options
General Preferences...
Mail and News Preferences...
Network Preferences...
Security Preferences...

✓ Show Toolbar
✓ Show Location
Show Directory Buttons

✓ Auto Load Images

Document Encoding ▶

Save Options

Figure 15.1 *Choose Network Preferences in the Options menu.*

The settings in the Network Preferences dialog box control how Netscape works over a network. To view the Network Preferences dialog box, choose Network Preferences in the Options menu **(Figure 15.1)**.

The Network Preferences dialog box has three tabs. Click a tab's title to make it active and access its settings. Each tab is described in detail on the following pages.

Once you've made the desired changes to the settings, click OK to save the changes. Click Cancel to close the dialog box without saving changes. Click Help to access the Netscape Help file.

Network Preferences

15

171

Cache

Click the Cache tab in the Network Preferences dialog box to change the settings for the Disk and Memory caches, to change the directory, and to decide how often Netscape should compare a page saved in Cache with the actual page on the server.

Disk Cache

Verify Document

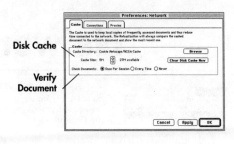

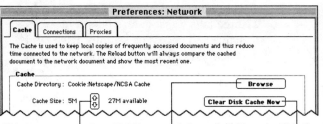

Click the arrows to set the size of the disk cache.

Click Browse and choose the folder where you want the disk cache to store the pages and images that you browse.

Click Clear Disk Cache Now to erase all the pages and images in the disk cache and make more space available on your hard disk.

Disk Cache

Netscape saves the pages and images that you browse in its disk cache. Once a page or image is stored in a cache, it takes much less time to display. Netscape organizes the cache when you exit the program. If it seems to take too long, try reducing the size of the disk cache.

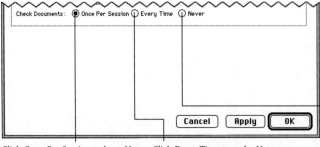

Click Once Per Session to have Netscape compare the cached version with the real page on the server only the first time you access the page during a session with Netscape.

Click Every Time to make Netscape compare the cached version with the server each time you browse the page. If you select this option, it doesn't make sense to have a big cache.

Click Never to have Netscape always use the cached version without checking for changes.

Verify Document

Pages on the Web are incredibly dynamic. Think of all the pages you've seen "under construction." You can have Netscape compare the document you have saved in cache with the current version once each time you open Netscape, every time you look at the page, or never.

Connections

Click the Connections tab in the Network preferences dialog box to define the number of connections that Netscape can make at one time, and to set the size of the network buffer.

Number of Connections

Network Buffer Size

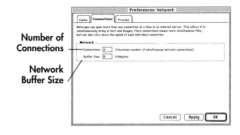

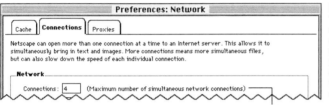

Type a number in the text box to determine how many connections Netscape should make at a time. The default is 4.

Number of Connections
The text and images on a page are distinct files on the server. Netscape can open more than one connection to the server in order to load the page more quickly, although the speed of each individual connection may deteriorate as a result.

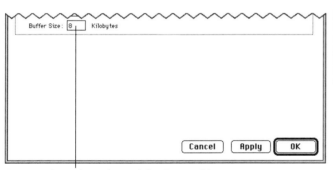

Network Buffer Size
The size of the network buffer determines the amount of data that can be received at a time. A larger number means more information can be received, but may saturate the computer.

Type a number in the text box to define the size of the network buffer.

Connections

Proxies

Click the Proxies tab in the Network preferences dialog box to change how Netscape interacts with proxy software. In situations where a firewall protects internal computer networks from external access, Netscape needs proxy software to get by the firewall to remote servers without compromising security.

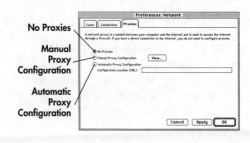

No Proxies

Manual Proxy Configuration

Automatic Proxy Configuration

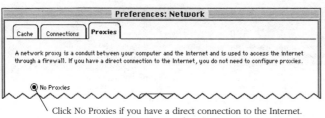

Click No Proxies if you have a direct connection to the Internet.

No Proxies
If your computer is not on a network and/or if you have a direct Internet connection, you don't have to worry about proxies at all and should choose No Proxies.

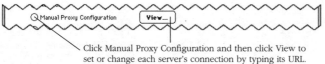

Click Manual Proxy Configuration and then click View to set or change each server's connection by typing its URL.

Manual Proxy Configuration
You can customize your own proxy configuration.

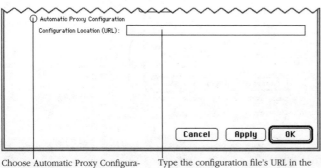

Choose Automatic Proxy Configuration if you have already set up a configuration file for connecting to different servers.

Type the configuration file's URL in the text box so that Netscape can find it.

Automatic Proxy Configuration
You can also set Netscape up to take advantage of an already constructed configuration file.

Security Preferences

Figure 16.1 *Choose Security Preferences in the Options menu.*

The settings in the Security Preferences dialog box help you protect your network, computer, or data. To access the dialog box, choose Security Preferences in the Options menu **(Figure 16.1)**.

The Security Preferences dialog box is divided into two sections called *tabs*. Click a tab's name to make it active and access its settings. Each tab is described in detail on the following pages.

Once you've made the desired changes to the security settings, click OK. Click Cancel to close the dialog box without saving the changes. Click Help to access the Netscape Help file.

General

Click the General tab in the Security preferences dialog box to disable Java and to determine when Netscape should alert you about the security status of certain areas or documents.

Java

Security Alerts

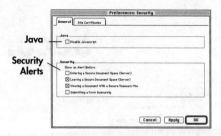

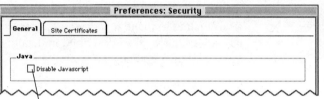

Click Disable Javascript so that Java applets do not run automatically.

Java

Since Java applets are applications running on your hard disk, they could conceivably be a security risk (i.e., if the program were malicious).

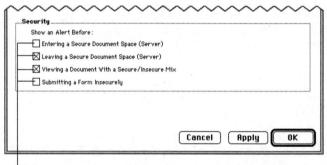

Check the situation in which you wish Netscape to alert you.

Security Alerts

You can have Netscape alert you of possible security problems. The individual alert boxes contain a "Show this Alert Next Time" button which, when unchecked, gives the same result as checking one of the options in this dialog box.

General

Site Certificates

Choose the Site Certificates tab in the Security preferences dialog box to change settings regarding site certificates. A site certificate indicates who operates the site, so that if you send information to them, you can be sure that they are who they say they are.

Site
Certificates

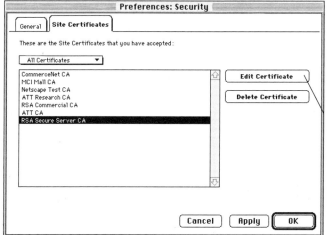

Site Certificates
You may receive various site certificates from companies that want to be able to securely identify themselves to you.

Click Edit Certificate to see the information in a site certificate and change its options.

Index

179

Index

Index

More from Peachpit Press

Animation and 3D Modeling on the Mac

Don and Melora Foley

The world isn't flat. Your animations needn't be, either. This visual, instructional volume guides experienced and novice animators through the exhilarating but complex challenge of designing in 3D. More than 1,000 striking, full-color illustrations demonstrate work from the world's best modelers and animators. Plus you'll learn the software you need most, including Director, Photoshop, Premiere, Infini-D, Ray Dream Designer, KPT Bryce, and more. *$34.95 (144 pages)*

Beyond the Mac is not a typewriter

Robin Williams

Think of this as the typography equivalent of Strunk and White's *The Elements of Style.* Expanding upon the content of its phenomenally popular predecessor *The Mac is not a typewriter*, this little book not only defines the principles governing type but explains the logic behind them, to help you see and understand what looks best and why. Armed with this knowledge, and putting into practice the secrets best-selling author Robin Williams reveals for making type readable and artistic, you can then go on to create beautiful, sophisticated, professional-looking pages on your computer. *$16.95 (224 pages)*

A Blip in the Continuum

Robin Williams

In this full-color book, author Robin Williams and illustrator John Tollett celebrate the new wave of type design known as grunge typography. Famous and not-so-famous quotes about type and design are set in a range of grunge fonts, using rule-breaking layouts, with illustrations created in Fractal Design Painter. The companion disk contains 22 freeware and shareware grunge fonts. *$22.95 (96 pages, w/disk)*

ColorCourse Interactive Training CDs

ColorExpert

ColorCourse/Photography demonstrates how to evaluate, scan, and separate photos for faithful reproduction. *ColorCourse/Illustration* covers trapping, scaling, blends, scanning specifications, and proofing. *ColorCourse/Imagesetting* focuses on getting the best final output possible with tips on topics like film imaging, proofing, quality assurance, and working with service bureaus. Includes a comprehensive trouble-shooting guide. Fully indexed with text links throughout. *$49.95 each (CD-ROM)*

A Day with Biff

Ron Romain and Joe Crabtree

It's a dog-eat-dog world. Just ask Biff, a protagonist pooch who's leapt paws first into the puzzling, amusing world of humans at work. Superb usable, original clip art makes this whimsical interactive book/disk package a joy. Like any good bad dog, Biff takes his job—distracting you from the task at hand—very seriously. His weapons: a maze, a treasure hunt, and more. Now play! *$24.95 (96 pages, w/disk)*

Director 4 for Macintosh: Visual QuickStart Guide

Andre Persidsky and Helmut Kobler

This guide teaches the fundamentals of using Director as well as the features new to this version. You'll learn how to animate text and graphics, use different Paint capabilities, alter color palettes, use sound, set scene transitions, add interactive controls to the movie, and much more. Like the other books in the *Visual QuickStart* series, *Director 4 for Macintosh* consists primarily of illustrations, with text playing a supporting role. It is organized as a reference rather than a tutorial so that you can quickly look up information on a particular tool or function. *$18.95 (248 pages)*

Everyone's Guide to Successful Publications

Elizabeth Adler

This comprehensive reference book pulls together all the information essential to developing and producing printed materials that will get your message across. Packed with ideas, practical advice, examples, and hundreds of photographs and illustrations, it discusses planning the printed piece, writing, design, desktop publishing, preparation for printing, and distribution. *$28 (416 pages)*

HTML: Visual QuickStart Guide

Elizabeth Castro

This step-by-step guide teaches you how to use Hypertext Markup Language to design pages for the World Wide Web. The book presumes no prior knowledge of HTML, or even the Internet, and uses clear, concise instructions for creating each element of a Web page. From the title and headers and your company's logo to complex tables and clickable graphics, this book covers it all. Because of its well-organized format, this book is also an excellent day-to-day reference for experienced Web designers. *$17.95 (176 pages)*

HyperCard 2.3 in a Hurry

George Beekman

HyperCard turns mere mortals into whiz-bang programmers. Witness Myst, which was created in HyperCard. Whether you're already building multimedia applications or just nosing your mouse into the introductory stacks, *HyperCard 2.3 in a Hurry* provides an easy-to-follow, self-paced tutorial that gets results fast. Entertaining projects help you master HyperCard's more advanced features. *$24.95 (384 pages)*

The Illustrator 5.0/5.5 Book

Deke McClelland

Experienced Illustrator users and novices alike will learn many helpful tips and techniques from this book. Thorough and comprehensive, *The Illustrator 5.0/5.5 Book* gives in-depth coverage of Illustrator's latest features. *$29.95 (688 pages)*

The Illustrator Wow! Book

Sharon Steuer

Modeled on the best-selling *Photoshop Wow! Book,* this book provides step-by-step descriptions with full-color illustrations of actual commercial art produced with Adobe Illustrator. The works of over 70 of the country's best Illustrator artists are included. A unique introductory chapter, "The Zen of Illustrator," helps you understand how the program thinks. The accompanying disk includes tutorials, special filters, artist tips, and other goodies. *$39.95 224 pages (w/ disk)*

The Mac is not a typewriter

Robin Williams

This best-selling, elegant guide to typesetting on the Mac has received rave reviews for its clearly presented information, friendly tone, and easy access. Twenty quick and easy chapters cover what you need to know to make your documents look clean and professional. *$9.95 (72 pages)*

The Official Photo CD Handbook: A Verbum Interactive Guide

Michael Gosney, et al.

With Photo CD, Kodak's breakthrough technology, you don't have to wait for tomorrow's electronic cameras to join the digital photography revolution. Learn how to use and store digital images and media files without spending a fortune. Two CDs include multimedia presentations, valuable Photo CD utilities, and 68MB of usable images, backgrounds, and sounds. *$39.95 (384 pages, w/2 CD-ROMs)*

Painter 3.1 For Macintosh: Visual QuickStart Guide

Elaine Weinmann and Peter Lourekas

Packed with illustrations created by the authors and 19 other accomplished artists, this book serves as a computer art class that inspires users to explore the many features of Painter 3.1. Like other books in the *Visual QuickStart* series, *Painter 3.1 for Macintosh* consists of numerous easy-to-follow steps that guide you through the program visually, showing you how to really use it. *$19.95 (256 pages)*

The Painter Wow! Book

Cher Threinen-Pendarvis and Jim Benson

Painter has so many features even power users don't know all the tricks. Whatever your skill level, you'll scurry to the computer to try out the examples in The Painter Wow! Book. This full-color volume uses hundreds of stunning, original illustrations depicting Painter's full range of styles and effects. Step-by-step descriptions clearly explain how each piece was created. The latest offering in the award-winning Wow! series. *$39.95 (224 pages w/CD-ROM)*

Photoshop 3 for Macintosh: Visual QuickStart Guide

Elaine Weinmann and Peter Lourekas

Completely revised for Photoshop 3, this indispensible guide is ideal for Mac users who want to get started in Adobe Photoshop without having to wade through long-winded explanations. *Photoshop 3 for Macintosh* uses illustrated, step-by-step examples to cover Photoshop fundamentals, including how to use masks, filters, colors, and more. *$19.95 (295 pages)*

The Photoshop 3 Wow! Book (Mac Edition)

Linnea Dayton and Jack Davis

This book is really two books in one: an easy-to-follow, step-by-step tutorial of Photoshop fundamentals, and over 150 pages of tips and techniques for getting the most out of Photoshop version 3. Full-color throughout, *The Photoshop Wow! Book* shows how professional artists make the best use of Photoshop. Includes a CD-ROM containing Photoshop filters and utilities. *$39.95 (286 pages, w/CD-ROM)*

Photoshop in Black and White, 2nd Edition

Jim Rich and Sandy Bozek

Covering both versions 2.5 and 3.0, this book explains how to adjust black-and-white images of any type for reproduction. Topics include image characteristics; adjusting highlights, shadows, and midtones; sharpening images; and converting from color to grayscale. Appendices cover scanning, resampling and calibration. *$18 (44 pages)*

The QuarkXPress Book, 4th Edition for Macintosh

David Blatner and Eric Taub

This is the highest rated, most comprehensive, and best-selling QuarkXPress book ever published. Now totally updated to cover the newest version, this book is made for easy access, including a handy tear-out keystroke shortcut card. You'll find valuable information on XTensions, EfiColor, AppleEvent scripting and more. Winner of the 1991 Benjamin Franklin Award (computer book category). *$29.95 (784 pages)*

QuarkXPress 3.3 for Macintosh: Visual QuickStart Guide

Elaine Weinmann

Winner of the Benjamin Franklin Award, this book is a terrific way to get introduced to QuarkXPress in just a couple of hours. Lots of illustrations and screen shots make each feature of the program absolutely clear. This book is helpful to both beginners and intermediate QuarkXPress users. *$15.95 (240 pages)*

Order Form

USA 800-283-9444 • 510-548-4393 • FAX 510-548-5991
CANADA 800-387-8028 • 416-447-1779 • FAX 800-456-0536 OR 416-443-0948

Qty	Title	Price	Total
	SUBTOTAL		
	ADD APPLICABLE SALES TAX*		
	SHIPPING		
	TOTAL		

Shipping is by UPS ground: $4 for first item, $1 each add'l.

*We are required to pay sales tax in all states with the exceptions of AK, DE, HI, MT, NH, NV, OK, OR, SC and WY. Please include appropriate sales tax if you live in any state not mentioned above.

Customer Information

NAME

COMPANY

STREET ADDRESS

CITY   STATE   ZIP

PHONE (   )   FAX (   )
[REQUIRED FOR CREDIT CARD ORDERS]

Payment Method

❑ CHECK ENCLOSED   ❑ VISA   ❑ MASTERCARD   ❑ AMEX

CREDIT CARD #   EXP. DATE

COMPANY PURCHASE ORDER #

Tell Us What You Think

PLEASE TELL US WHAT YOU THOUGHT OF THIS BOOK: TITLE:_____

WHAT OTHER BOOKS WOULD YOU LIKE US TO PUBLISH?

MAC   **PEACHPIT PRESS** • 2414 Sixth Street • Berkeley, CA 94710